...ONE ASTER BOUVARDIA C...
...NTHEMUM CORNF... CO...
...NIUM FREESIA GARDENIA GE...
...HYACINTH HYDRANGEA IRIS...
...Y PHLOX RANUNCULUS ROS...
...ER SWEET PEA TUBEROSE TU...
...RIA AMARYLLIS ANEMONE AS...
...ON CHRYSANTHEMUM CORN...
...SY DELPHINIUM FREESIA GAR...
...HYACINTH HYDRANGEA IRIS...
...Y PHLOX RANUNCULUS ROS...
...ER SWEET PEA TUBEROSE TU...
...RIA AMARYLLIS ANEMONE AS...
...ON CHRYSANTHEMUM CORN...
...SY DELPHINIUM FREESIA GAR...
...HYACINTH HYDRANGEA IRIS...

the knot BOOK OF WEDDING FLOWERS

the knot BOOK OF
WEDDING FLOWERS

CARLEY RONEY

CHRONICLE BOOKS
SAN FRANCISCO

Library of Congress Cataloging-in-
Publication Data available.

ISBN 0-8118-3263-5

Manufactured in China
Designed by Frances Baca

Distributed in Canada
by Raincoast Books
9050 Shaughnessy Street
Vancouver, British Columbia v6p 6e5

10 9 8 7 6 5 4 3 2

Chronicle Books LLC
85 Second Street
San Francisco, California 94105

www.chroniclebooks.com

*Page 2: A monochromatic bouquet
plays with hue and texture. This
dramatic example in lavender
combines 'Sterling Silver' roses,
thistle, and agapanthus.*

ACKOWLEDGMENTS

My deepest appreciation goes to Jennifer Cegielski, whose vision, enthusiasm, and hours of attention are truly responsible for the quality of this book.

Other key members of The Knot team contributed to this beautiful book as a labor of love: Thanks to Brittany O'Neil, for acting as photo-shoot team captain to on-set stylist; to Rachel Kashon, for lending her artistic vision to the photography; to Amy Elliott, for her can-do attitude and ability to get things done; to Julie Raimondi, for pinch-hitting with aplomb; and to Fred Seelig and Amy Nathanson, for making sure the facts were checked and the copy was sound. And, of course, thanks to my agents, Jonathan Diamond and Jennifer Unter.

In addition to the in-house team here at The Knot, I am grateful for the inspiring images of primary photographer Wendell Webber. Thanks also to photographers Paul Costello, Troy House, and Cristina Tarantola for allowing their photos to appear in this book. Thanks, too, to the team at Soho Studios, and big thanks to Wearkstatt for lending us their perfect gowns. And a special thank-you to Denise Ono, our delightful model, whose arms never tired from holding bouquets.

As evidenced by the exquisite work shown in this book, there are many talented New York florists and event planners to thank for their artistic vision and ability to wow us with every creation: the talented and ever enthusiastic Peter Krask, who has been helping us since the beginning of our floral endeavors; Elizabeth Ryan, for the innumerable, stunning bouquets she created for the cover shot; our "four seasons" florists Renny Reynolds (spring), Michael George (summer), Saundra Parks of Daily Blossom (fall), and Preston Bailey (winter); plus the florists at Bloom, Botanica, Color of Magic, Leslie Palme Event Design, Lotus NYC, Mandana, Matthew David Events, Ltd., Quade, Rebecca Cole, Jen Stone and the team at stonekelly, Susan Holland, and V.S.F. Thanks also to flower wholesaler Gary Page and to the many floral professionals and event planners around the country who contributed their knowledge to the information in this book: Avi Adler and David Stark of Avi Adler; Brit Woods of Flowers From the Woods; Dean Andreadas of Forever in Bloom; Eileen Lamoureaux of Grassroots; J. K. Homer of Through the Grapevine; Joyce Scardina Becker of Events of Distinction; Katie Fechter of Details; Ken Puttbach of Botanicals; Melissa Paul of Melissa Paul, Ltd.; Meredith Perez Waga of Belle Fleur; and Nina Nichols Austin.

Finally, we send our gratitude to our editor at Chronicle Books, Mikyla Bruder, whose vision provided sound guidance and insight at every turn. And to Ben Shaykin and the design team at Chronicle, thank you for transforming our words and pictures into a work of art.

As always, love and thanks to our friends and families for their unending patience and support.

CONTENTS

Introduction 7

CHAPTER ONE
THE FLOWERS 11

Wedding Flowers A to Z 13
Beyond Flowers 49
Color Palettes. 51
    White 51
    Pink. 52
    Red and Orange 55
    Blue and Purple 56
    Yellow and Green 59

CHAPTER TWO
GETTING STARTED 61

Practical Considerations 62
Style Considerations 67
Finding a Florist 69
Doing It Yourself 75
Wedding Flower Timeline. 78
Wedding Flower Worksheet 80

CHAPTER THREE
BOUQUETS AND PERSONAL FLOWERS ...83

The Bridal Bouquet 84
Bouquet Portraits 89
Glossary of Bouquet Shapes 94
The Boutonniere 100
Bridesmaids' Bouquet 106
Flower Girls' Blooms 110
Corsages 113

CHAPTER FOUR
CENTERPIECES AND DECORATIONS 115

The Centerpiece 116
Centerpiece Portraits. 119
Glossary of Centerpiece
    Shapes and Styles 124
Scene Setters 130

CHAPTER FIVE
PUTTING IT ALL TOGETHER. 141

Wedding Portraits 142
The Big Day 159
Wedding Day Floral Timeline . . . 161

Quick Reference Flower Chart 162
Preserving Your Bouquet 166
Resources 167
Bibliography 170
Index 172
Credits 175

Flowers are

a given, a necessity, at weddings. Have you ever stopped to wonder why? Not merely decorative, wedding flowers are rich in symbolism, tradition, ritual, and pageantry that originated in ancient times and continue to be meaningful today.

The ancient Greeks and Romans utilized flowers and herbs in times of celebration. Greek brides wore wreaths or garlands made of mint and marigold, which were thought to be aphrodisiacs, while Roman brides held sheaves of wheat, which were believed to ensure fertility. The tradition of the bridal bouquet has its origins in the cluster of herbs an ancient Greek bride carried to ward off evil spirits. Once safely in the arms of her beloved, the bride tossed her bouquet to a lady in waiting, to spread her good fortune (the precursor to the modern-day bouquet toss). Also in ancient times, young girls often walked ahead of the bride, sprinkling herbs in her path to ensure her fertility; during the Elizabethan era girls scattered flower petals in the bride's path (the Renaissance version of today's flower girl).

In the Middle Ages, ladies anxiously welcomed their knights home from the Crusades by decorating their towns and homes with garlands, and they strewed fragrant plants and herbs about wedding sites to perfume the air. Individual flowers began to take on symbolic meaning, both religious and secular; Catholics associated white lilies with virginity, and poets and artists (ever the romantics) linked roses with love and desire.

In the 1630s, floriculture surged throughout Europe—"tulipomania" swept the continent as the Dutch export became available. While only the wealthy could afford them, flowers began to have more of a presence in general society. In the 1800s, the commercial flower trade was in full force, with Paris at its center. Flowers became a tool for communication and a means of expressing emotion in the "language of flowers" that developed during this time. Numerous books were written giving meanings to specific flower varieties and colors. Victorian society embraced this romantic concept wholeheartedly, and people used flowers to court each other and express ardor that might otherwise have been forbidden by the strict mores of the day. In the "language of flowers," a lilac was not just a lilac; it represented "the first emotions of love," and a young man might have given it to a woman in hopes of winning her affection. The lady, in response, might have carried daisies, signifying that she shared his sentiments. The boutonniere, a flower worn on a gentleman's lapel, also came into fashion during this time and was worn as an indicator of the gentleman's social standing.

The practice of carrying or wearing specific flower varieties at weddings can be traced to the marriage of England's Queen Victoria and Prince Albert in 1840. The queen not only set the standard of the white wedding gown, she also adorned both her dress and her hair with fresh orange blossoms. Photographs of the wedding appeared in newspapers, and soon brides everywhere were seeking the flower to wear at their own weddings. At this time the Industrial Revolution was starting, and steam engines began transporting flowers from country to country, introducing previously unavailable flowers to new locations and opening up a new world of flower choices to brides.

The 1930s saw the birth of the celebrity florist. In London, the sophisticated designs of Constance Spry attracted the city's leading figures and secured her position as the florist for the controversial wedding of King Edward VIII and Wallis Simpson in 1937. With her innovative approach, Spry inspired trends across the globe and set the stage for the modern-day florist. No longer just vendors who hocked their bushels of roses, florists became creative celebrities and trend makers, a must for the society bride.

During the Second World War, flower production came to a virtual standstill; farmers needed to plant crops instead of gardens, and brides were forced to walk

Overleaf: The bridal bouquet is the focal point for all of the other flowers for a wedding. Here, luscious peonies set the style with their soft pink color and abundant, girlish blooms.

down the aisle holding fabric flowers. However, with the war also came the modernization of the airplane and the widespread use of refrigeration, which soon led to the dawn of global floral trading. With the largest flower market in the world at Aalsmeer, Holland became the capital of flower distribution worldwide, importing and exporting billions of blooms grown in Europe, South America, Africa, and the United States. These days, computerized auctions, growing innovations, and revolutionary packaging materials make it possible for brides to choose from thousands of flowers, year-round, from practically anywhere in the world.

As a result of the astounding number of varieties available, selecting flowers for your wedding can be somewhat overwhelming. Where to begin? With the flowers themselves. In Chapter 1 you'll learn about some of the most popular wedding flowers. Once you've gotten to know these beauties, you'll find out how to identify your own wedding-flower style and get started planning your flowers in Chapter 2. We'll also provide tips for finding the right florist, and advice for doing your own wedding flowers if you so choose. In Chapter 3 you'll learn about personal flowers, such as bouquets, boutonnieres, corsages, and blooms for flower girls. We'll describe the standard shapes of these arrangements and how you can adapt them to match your style, as well as how to make all of these corresponding elements work together. In Chapter 4 we'll move on to flowers for your ceremony and reception, including centerpieces, decorations, and flower-inspired favors to help you and your guests celebrate in style. Then, in Chapter 5 we'll show you bouquets, boutonnieres, centerpieces, decorations, and more for four distinct weddings, and we'll provide a timeline of the flower-related events that will take place on your own big day. We'll even give you information on preserving your bouquet. Finally, our useful Resources section will offer a complete wedding-flower chart of essential details and an address book of helpful flower professionals.

Ready to take a walk through a garden of wedding flowers? Let's go.

1 THE FLOWERS

WEDDING FLOWERS A TO Z

BEYOND FLOWERS

COLOR PALETTES

Left: A small nosegay of lily of the valley is a popular choice for brides because of the flower's distinctive perfume.

Picture yourself walking through a glorious garden with every flower at its peak. Which would you pick? Something commonplace? Something colorful? The rarest? The most fragrant? As you probably already know, flowers come in thousands of varieties. To help you narrow down your list of choices, in this chapter we offer an overview of more than fifty of the most popular wedding flowers. We've arranged the flowers alphabetically and highlighted a few all-time bridal favorites, including the rose, the tulip, the lily, and the orchid. All you need to do is decide which particular blooms appeal to you. Some varieties will catch your eye with their silhouette or delicate details, some with their brilliant color or unusual texture. Others might stand out because of their intoxicating scent, or because of a Victorian meaning that echoes a quality in your relationship. For additional help, turn to the flower chart on page 162, which provides basic information for each flower (season, colors, scent, and cost).

Choosing the flowers for your wedding is a practical process, but it's also an instinctual one—you will know what you like when you see it. You may already have a sense of what you want, perhaps an idea as broad as a color theme ("only pink"), or as precise as a particular bloom ("only roses"). But whether you're a flower fanatic or neophyte, be sure to keep an open mind as you go about your dreaming—you may discover new varieties you have never considered before. As you flip through these pages, make a note of the blooms that speak to you. Each flower has its own distinctive attributes, and each will bring something different to your wedding.

Wedding Flowers A to Z

Alstroemeria

Amaryllis

Anemone

Greek mythology is the source of two legends about the anemone.

Also known as the Peruvian lily, the alstroemeria's bright, small blooms grow in clusters and often have freckled petals. They are moderately priced and are best used as a backdrop to primary flowers, although a mass of pink alstroemeria makes a lovely and cost-effective bouquet. Their colors include white, yellow, pink, orange, and red.

Brides desiring maximum impact might choose this impressive flower, which features two to five large, trumpet-shaped blooms that open in succession at the top of its extra-long stalk. Grown from a large bulb, the amaryllis has its origins in the tropical rainforests of Africa and South America and is now available in white, pale yellow, pale green, pink, salmon, and red. Very rare and expensive, these flowers are long-lasting and offer a lot of drama with just a few stems.

Opposite: These jewel-toned flowers were said to have sprung up from the blood that was shed by Aphrodite's lover, Adonis, when he died. The ancient Greeks also believed that Zephyrus, god of the west wind, favored the bloom, hence its other name, windflower. While not scented, this relative of the peony and ranunculus is sought after for its vibrant magenta, red, and purple hues. Just a few bright blooms add a blast of color to bouquets and arrangements.

Bouvardia

Aster

According to mythology, the starburst-shaped aster originated when Virgo scattered stardust on the earth. A good supporting-role flower, the aster is available in white, pink, hot pink, lavender, red, and purple. The daisylike flowers are a charming background for showier blooms.

The lovely bouvardia is just perfect for fleshing out a classic wedding bouquet or arrangement. With its clusters of small, star-shaped blossoms bursting up from leafy green stems, the delicate bouvardia is useful for fleshing out a classic wedding bouquet or arrangement. Peaking in summer and fall, it can be found in white, pink, peach, and red.

Calla Lily

Also known as the arum lily, this trumpet-shaped blossom originated in Africa and symbolized "magnificent beauty" to the Victorians.

Opposite: The calla lily's distinctive form has been depicted in Art Nouveau and Art Deco works as well as twentieth-century photography. Two types are commonly available: one with a large head and a long, smooth stem, suitable for tall arrangements or presentation bouquets, and a miniature version ideal for nosegays and boutonnieres. Creamy ivory is the most popular color, but calla lilies also come in yellow, orange, mauve-pink, and dark purple.

Camellia

A symbol of perfect loveliness and beauty, this multipetaled relative of the tea plant was originally cultivated by the Chinese. The flower had a notable role in Verdi's opera *La Traviata,* which he adapted from the play *The Lady of the Camellias*. In the story, a courtesan named Violetta always wears a white camellia, except for the few days of the month when she is "not available" and dons a red camellia instead. The flower comes in white, cream, pinks, and reds.

Carnation

Don't turn up your nose at the common carnation. Affordable, plentiful, and available year-round, this long-lasting flower is full of possibilities for weddings.

Opposite: The ruffled-heads look offers an inexpensive way to bring lushness and color to bouquets and arrangements. When massed, they also make a pretty—and inexpensive—bouquet of their own. Carnations have a long history; they were reportedly used to make ceremonial crowns in ancient Greece, and they were on hand at the wedding of Maximilian of Austria, the emperor of Mexico (1864–67), as a symbol of marital bliss. Today, more than three hundred species, in large, single blooms and miniature spray varieties, are available. Carnations are grown in a wide array of colors, with the most popular hues being in the pink, red, and burgundy family. Some have a lovely clovelike fragrance.

Chrysanthemum

About a thousand varieties of the long-lasting, versatile mum are grown, in single blossoms or sprays. The mum has been cultivated in the Far East for more than two thousand five hundred years, even appearing in the writings of Confucius. What it lacks in sweet perfume—its scent is strong and earthy—it makes up for in a range of bold colors. Several shades are available, including cream, yellow, chartreuse, red, and russet. Shown here, the white pompom mum and yellow spider mum are two of the many varieties.

Cornflower

In medieval lore, it was thought that a girl who placed a cornflower beneath her skirt could have any bachelor she desired—which is perhaps how the flower acquired its other name, bachelor's button. An inexpensive choice that is appropriate for a casual wedding, the cornflower comes in white, pink, dark magenta, and, most commonly, blue, with feathery blue-gray foliage. Its button head, and its colorful legend, make it a charming boutonniere flower for groomsmen.

Cosmos

Brides hoping to capture the look of a summer garden in full bloom would succeed with a choice of cosmos.

This inexpensive to moderately priced daisylike flower grows in shades of pink and magenta on long stems with feathery foliage. A striking chocolate color is also available and can be used to create rich late-summer arrangements.

Daffodil

Shakespeare and Wordsworth both waxed rhapsodic about this humble bulb flower. Perhaps it is so well liked because its merry yellow bloom is one of the first to appear after winter's frost subsides. The daffodil (and members of its family, including the narcissus and the jonquil) is a flower of true variety—blooms can be single or multiple, with large or small cups, in solid colors or in combinations of white and yellow with touches of orange. Some are scented, the paperwhite narcissus being the most fragrant and well known. Generally inexpensive, the daffodil makes a good wedding flower, because of its meaning, "regard and respect." Shown here, a dome of miniature daffodils is a fragrant spring bouquet.

Dahlia

Daisy

Delphinium and Larkspur

These bold, bushy flowers possess a history as dramatic as their appearance. Conquistadors found the dahlia in the gardens of the Aztecs and caused a sensation when they brought the flower back to Europe. As the dahlia gained popularity, the pursuit of its potatolike tubers was conducted with intrigue and deception—dahlia tubers were reportedly stolen even from the garden of the Empress Josephine! An inexpensive summer-through-early-fall choice, the dahlia has a peppery, earthy scent and is available in an array of flamboyant yellow, orange, pink, red, and purple hues.

The Victorian meaning of this cheery yellow-eyed flower is "innocence."

You might find the daisy a fitting flower for your wedding if you plucked its white petals in a game of "he loves me, he loves me not" as a child. Folklore has it that a daisy placed in a bride's left stocking ensures pregnancy early in the marriage. Generally available year-round, the affordable daisy is a lovely and whimsical flower for an informal wedding.

A classic in English cottage flower beds, the delphinium has towering spires and clustered florets. The delphinium and its similar spiky sister, the larkspur (not shown), lend a country-garden feel to wedding arrangements while adding height and drama. Also available in white and pink, they are most spectacular in blues and purples—Wedgwood blue, mauve, violet, and dark sapphire colors are available. Delphiniums can be found year-round, but most colors are at their peak from summer to early fall. Larkspur thrives from early to mid-summer.

Freesia

A favorite of perfumers for its fresh, fruity scent, freesia packs a lot of fragrance in just a few blossoms. A couple of stems are all that's needed to make a bouquet sweet-smelling. Available in white, yellow, red, and purple, freesia smells strongest in its deeper colors. The green buds clustered along the thin, arched stem open gradually into delicate flowers.

Gardenia

Surrounded by dark green, waxy leaves, the exquisite gardenia exudes a very sultry and heavy scent.

Opposite: It was this intoxicating fragrance that captivated an English sea captain traveling through South Africa in 1754, prompting him to bring home one of the native plants as a souvenir. But the delicate, creamy ivory petals of this expensive flower can bruise easily so handle with care. Fragrant gardenias have many uses—carry a few as a posy, wear one as a corsage, or float a few in a low bowl for a minimalist centerpiece. Large three- to four-inch blossoms, as well as a miniature variety, are available.

Gerbera

This graphic flower is so flawless in its form that it almost doesn't look real. But, fortunately for us, it is. Born in the hottest climates of Asia and Africa, the gerbera is a year-round gem that comes in a crayon-box range of colors—nearly 350 intense shades are available, including bright orange, pink, and red, plus yellow and burgundy. This cheery bloom was considered a symbol of friendship by the Victorians.

Gladiolus

Grape Hyacinth

Hyacinth

In ancient mythology Hyacinthus was a figure in a tale of tragic love.

Standing tall and proud, the gladiolus is a spiky stem with large florets that open in succession; miniature varieties with fewer florets are also available. Full stems can be used to add height to arrangements, while the individual florets can be made into boutonnieres. Many of its varieties originated on the African continent. The flower's name is derived from the Latin for sword (*gladius*), after the shape of its leaves. Look for gladiolus in a wide spectrum of colors—white, yellow, orange, magenta, lavender, and red—including some varieties with bicolor flowers.

Grape hyacinth gets its name from the shape of its flower, and perhaps its mild, sweet scent. Its cone-shape resembles a miniature bunch of grapes perched upside down on its slender green stem. Sometimes called muscari, it is available in greenish white but is most often seen in a pretty purplish blue. This springtime bulb flower can be expensive, so it is best used as an accent or massed in small bunches.

Opposite: Today we know this stocky bulb flower as a fragrant signature of spring. The hyacinth is cultivated in white and in intense and pastel shades of pink, blue, and purple. Its scent is strong, so just a few flowers are needed to make their presence known in centerpieces or arrangements.

Iris

Lilac

Hydrangea

With its big, bushy head and intense colors, it's no wonder the hydrangea represented "vanity" in the language of flowers.

The color of one of the most popular varieties changes from bubble-gum pink to sky blue, depending on the acid level of the soil. Other popular shades include burgundy and white. A stem or two of this moderately priced, scentless shrub flower helps fill out arrangements and bouquets.

This unusually shaped flower has been admired by many throughout history. Ancient Greeks associated it with their gods, and ancient Egyptians linked it to their pharaohs; to the medieval Europeans, it signified chivalry and served as the model for the French fleur-de-lis symbol. Painters like Monet and Van Gogh, too, were captivated by its image. Myth and majesty aside, the three most common varieties are the Dutch iris (shown), the graceful Siberian iris, and the large "bearded" iris, all grown in numerous shades of white, yellow, and purple.

Prized for its soft perfume, the lilac flourished in Turkey and was introduced to Europe by the French. Although they are the products of a long-living tree, the lilac's grapelike clusters of tiny flowers have a short life after being cut, so they are used sparingly at weddings. The lilac is at its peak in spring, and single- and double-flowered varieties come in white, pink, lavender, and purple.

The Lily

While the lily is available in many colors, the pristine white version holds the most significance for a bride.

Often referred to as "the Queen of Flowers," the glamorous lily can definitely make you feel like a member of royalty if you carry it on your wedding day. It has been associated with godliness, and to numerous societies it has represented purity, fruitfulness, and youthful innocence—not bad qualities to embody (even if just for the wedding day). The white lily carries a great deal of religious symbolism, especially in its many relationships to sacred female figures. In tales of Greek mythology, the flowers were said to have sprouted from the ground where the breast milk of the goddess Hera had fallen. In Christian circles, the lily has been linked with the Virgin Mary. The classic, enduring white lily is thought to have existed since the end of the Ice Age.

With three to seven flower heads on a single stem and a moderate price, the lily offers a lot of value for its cost, and it is generally available year-round. It also comes in many forms—the blooms can be star-shaped or trumpet-shaped, with plain, striped, or spotted petals, in white, yellow, orange, pink, or red. Keep in mind that no flower is perfect, and the lily is, of course, no exception. One of its pros is also one of its cons: its strong, heavy smell can be seductive to some while outright irritating to others. In addition, if the flower is left intact its stamens shed pollen that can stain anything they touch (your gown, your hands, the tablecloths, and so on), so it's best to have the stamens removed. There are four lily types that savvy brides might consider: Oriental, Asiatic, longiflorum, and gloriosa.

Left: With its large, star-shaped blooms, these flamboyant, fragrant oriental lilies make quite a statement.

FEATURE FLOWER The Lily

1 Asiatic Lily

When you picture a lily, you are most likely envisioning the Asiatic variety, which are the ones usually found at your local florist or grocer. The long stems of these lilies are abundant with blossoms that burst with vivid color. Asiatic lilies are less expensive than the Oriental variety, but their flowers are also smaller and grow closer together; as a result, they're an excellent choice for large, compact bouquets.

2 Longiflorum Lily

This pure-white, extremely fragrant flower is commonly known as the Easter lily. Its large, trumpet-shaped blossoms are depicted in medieval religious paintings; due to the flower's association with the Virgin Mary, it is also known as the Madonna lily. A native of Japan, the longiflorum lily was first brought to America in 1919. Today, very few growers produce this flower, and it is available for only limited periods during the year.

3 Gloriosa Lily

While technically not of the lily family (it grows on a climbing vine, not from a bulb), this flower's reflexed petals and stamens bear a resemblance to those of true lilies. Generally pinkish red tipped with yellow, the gloriosa, or Rothschild lily, adds tropical punch to bouquets and arrangements.

4 Oriental Lily

Oriental lilies grow fewer blossoms than Asiatic lilies, and, though pricier, only a couple of stems are needed to make a big impact. Oriental lilies grow in shades of pink and red, but the most notable for brides is the white 'Casablanca,' which is very long lasting and fragrant.

1 2

3 4

Lily
of the Valley

Their fresh, perfumelike scent is unmistakable, and it's hard to believe such a delicious fragrance can come from such tiny flowers.

With its bell-shaped florets dangling from a thin stem, the lily of the valley is sometimes called "the ladder to heaven." In Norse mythology, the flower is linked to Ostara, the goddess of springtime, and while most plentiful during this season, it remains available—and very expensive—year-round. While most people only know of the white lily of the valley, there also exists a very rare rosy pink variety.

Lisianthus

Opposite: This cupped flower somewhat resembles a rose or ranunculus that is missing a few petals. Lisianthus, which signifies "showiness," boasts multiple blossoms and buds on a single stem and a somewhat peppery scent. Its year-round availability, moderate price, and good range of colors, including white, peach, pink, and purple, make it an excellent choice as a secondary flower for bouquets and arrangements.

The Orchid

Sexy and exquisitely gorgeous, the orchid is a star at any wedding.

When it comes to choosing a wedding flower, it's hard to argue against one that symbolizes ecstasy. To be frank, the sultry orchid has always been associated with sex. The look of its flowers is unmistakably erotic, and its very name comes from the Greek word for testicle (*orchis*), thanks to the appearance of its tubers. Some orchid varieties are even labeled after parts of the female anatomy—witness 'ladies' fingers' and 'ladies' tresses'. Throughout history, sensual side effects have even been attributed to the ingestion of the orchid's parts. A botanical tome of 1640 advises, "if a man ate a large orchid tuber, he would beget many children," and the flavoring found in the seed pods of the vanilla orchid has been considered an aphrodisiac since as far back as 1753.

The orchid dates to the age of the dinosaurs and thrives in tropical rain forests. Thousands of species are cultivated worldwide, which means there is an orchid for every type of bride. Orchids, diverse in color and fragrance, grow as individual blooms or multiple flowers on a stem. They are surprisingly hardy and hold up well (even without water), which makes them quite wedding-friendly. A full spray of orchids can be used in bouquets and arrangements, or a single blossom can be plucked to make an exotic boutonniere. You could spend a lifetime sifting through the thousands of orchid options available, but four main types are commonly used at weddings: cymbidium, dendrobium, oncidium, and phalaenopsis. They range in price from moderate to very expensive, and, for the most part, they are available year-round.

Left: Chartreuse cymbidium orchids take center stage in this green-themed bouquet.

1 Cymbidium Orchid

A standard cymbidium orchid boasts several large flowers per stem. Once cut, these fragrant beauties remain quite durable, which makes them an excellent choice for corsages. Cymbidium orchids can perish in colder temperatures, so pass on them if the temperature on your wedding day will be on the cooler side. Available in a range of colors including white, green, yellow, pink, red, and rust, the cymbidium is one of the more expensive orchids.

2 Dendrobium Orchid

The sweet-scented dendrobiums comprise the second-largest class of orchids. The most common commercial variety has several small blossoms on a single stem. The dendrobium comes in white, cream, yellow, orange, pink, red, lavender, and purple, and their long stems make them a good addition to cascade bouquets or tall arrangements.

3 Oncidium Orchid

Oncidiums are often referred to as spray orchids, since most varieties have slender, branching sprays of flowers with flaring petals and ruffled lips. Their tiny blossoms add bits of color when arranged with other flowers. Oncidium orchids are most often grown in Mexico and on the islands of the Caribbean. They are available in yellow, red, reddish brown, and, less commonly, in white and in pink.

4 Phalaenopsis Orchid

The ancient Greeks named this orchid after the moth, perhaps because its flowers sway from the stem or maybe because the wide, flat petals resemble open wings. Whatever the reason, the moniker stuck, and the phalaenopsis is now also known as the moth orchid. Although it is one of the more expensive orchids, the phalaenopsis is long-lasting and should survive through the day without wilting. A single stem will have a few blossoms at different stages of development. White and pink tones are most common, although shades of yellow, red, and green are also available; many phalaenopsis orchids are dotted or striped.

1 2

3 4

Peony

Phlox

Ranunculus

To carry these flowers is to tell your partner, "I am dazzled by your charms."

The peony is showy in its lush and full-headed structure, sweet perfume, and bright color. Despite this, the flower acquired the meaning "bashfulness." Cultivated in Asia for more than a thousand years and developed further by the French, the peony is a cherished wedding flower. A relative of the ranunculus and the anemone, the peony is available in two main types, the herbaceous and the tree peony (the latter flowers do not last as long when cut). Grown in single- and double-flowered styles, this expensive flower is seasonally available from late spring to early summer, but can be imported in the fall.

Perhaps phlox's popularity at weddings is due to its meaning, "unification of the souls." These dainty white, pink, or purple flowers originated in North America, where they are a backyard staple. With large clusters of small-petaled, disk-shaped blossoms atop branching stems, phlox provides a lush backdrop for featured flowers in a bouquet or arrangement.

Opposite: Looking for a cost-effective alternative to the rose and the peony? Try the lush, multipetaled ranunculus, a relative of the buttercup. This flower was first seen by Westerners in the Far East around the thirteenth century. Available in practically every color, the mild-scented ranunculus features several blossoms on a stem with fernlike foliage.

FEATURE FLOWER

The Rose

Is it any wonder that roses rank as the most beloved of wedding flowers?

Long considered a symbol of beauty and love, the rose has captivated commoners and royalty alike. Legend has it that Nero required rose petals to be strewn at his feet and wore wreaths of roses at his many weddings, and that Cleopatra seduced both Julius Caesar and Marc Antony with the flower. The rose figures in many a myth and fairy tale, and romantic writers and poets have used the flower as a metaphor for emotion, beauty, passion, and true love.

If you believed Gertrude Stein, you might think that a rose is a rose is a rose. In fact, there are more than three thousand commercially grown varieties of roses, with many available year-round. Their accessibility means that roses can be surprisingly affordable. However, the price of roses goes up around key flower-giving holidays such as Valentine's Day and Mother's Day—so if your wedding date is near one of these holidays, you may wish to rethink your flower choice. And although you may associate the rose with a luxurious fragrance, not every rose is scented.

Always popular, roses are far from boring, particularly when it comes to color. Some, such as the all-white 'Virginia', are a single, solid color. Others are bicolor, like the 'Leonidas', which is a copper hue accented with russet. There are striped roses, such as the famous garnet-striped 'Rosa Mundi', and tipped roses, like the yellow 'Peace', edged with pink.

Three main types of roses are likely candidates for your wedding flowers: hybrid tea roses, spray roses, and garden roses.

Right: A bouquet of roses, either in a single shade or mixed, is one of the most classic a bride can carry. This dome mixes 'Elize', 'Sahara', and bicolor 'Leonidas' varieties.

The Meaning of Roses

In the Victorian "language of flowers," each color carried a specific meaning:

CORAL: desire

LAVENDER: enchantment

ORANGE: fascination

PALE PINK: grace

RED: true love, beauty and deep, passionate love

WHITE: purity

WHITE AND RED: unity

YELLOW: friendship

1 2

3 4

FEATURE FLOWER The Rose

1 & 2 Hybrid Tea Rose

Falling under the horticultural classification known as modern roses, the hybrid teas are the ones you generally see at your local florist. The 'Black Magic' rose (no. 1) is sought after for its rich deep color. Bicolor roses like the russet 'Leonidas' (no. 2) offer variations of hue and add visual interest to arrangements. Hybrid tea roses have been flourishing since their inception in 1867. They have the classic rose shape, featuring medium to large heads with high, pointy centers and long stems. Grown commercially in environmentally controlled hothouses, they are valued for their uniformity, durability, and global availability. Most have only a subtle scent or none at all. These flowers will last through the day without wilting or bruising. With a moderate price for most of the year, hybrid tea roses are an excellent wedding choice.

If you want to build your wedding flowers around a single color or a palette, consider the hybrid tea roses that come in your chosen color. We've compiled some popular varieties by color in the following list. However, as you learn about the different varieties, try not to become too attached to a specific one, since it may not be available or at its peak around your wedding. When your wedding approaches, you will want the variety that is at its peak.

CREAM/WHITE: 'Bianca', 'Virginia', 'Vendela'
LAVENDER: 'Blue Bird', 'Silver Cloud', 'Sterling Silver'
ORANGE: 'Miracle', 'Sari', 'Spicy'
PEACH: 'Eva', 'Surprise', 'Versillia'
PINK (DEEP): 'Bolero', 'Orlando', 'Souvenir'
PINK (PALE): 'Amorosa', 'Charming Unique', 'Veronica'
RED (CLASSIC): 'Carmen', 'Classy', 'Red Devil'
RED (DARK): 'Black Magic', 'Carte Noir', 'Deep Secret'
YELLOW: 'Aalsmeer Gold', 'Lemon Dream', 'Skyline'
BICOLOR: 'Anna' (cream and soft pink), 'Fancy Amazon' (cream and red), 'Laguna' (cream and deep pink), 'Leonidas' (russet and gold)

3 Spray Rose

With as many as five to ten small heads on each stem, spray roses appear more natural and garden-grown than do single-headed hybrid tea roses (even though both are commercially produced). Because the stems have multiple heads, spray roses can fill out a bouquet or arrangement with fewer stems than with hybrid tea roses. Available in single-hue as well as bicolor varieties, spray roses can be mixed and matched with hybrid teas in complementary colors.

4 Garden Rose

Don't ignore these beauties simply because of their alternate name, old-fashioned roses. Rare garden roses, such as the dark pink 'Wimi' shown here, open fully and have a classic rose scent. By strict definition, an old garden rose is one that belongs to a class that existed before 1867, but you can identify them by their bushy, open heads. These roses prosper in the summer months and are more fragile than hybrid teas. And although they emit a sweet scent, they'll wallop your wallet while charming your nose—be prepared to pay a high price for these fragrant, rare blooms.

Stephanotis

Stock

Scabiosa

It's not hard to understand how the scabiosa, with its tufted head atop a long, wiry stem, got its other name, pin cushion. This enchanting, scentless flower is right at home tucked between showier blooms. It is most often seen in white, pink, lavender, purple, or burgundy.

The meaning given to the stephanotis is "marital happiness," making the flower an obvious choice for weddings.

The stephanotis is mildly scented and available year-round. The star-shaped, waxy florets actually grow on a flowering vine; each must be individually wired or placed onto a special holder before it can be used in a bouquet or boutonniere.

Rising on a tall stem, stock has dense clusters of small single- or double-blossomed flowers. Stock first became known outside of the Mediterranean region toward the end of the Middle Ages. An inexpensive flower that is available year-round, stock is valued for its use as a complementary flower and its fragrant, spicy clovelike scent. Look for it in white, pink, apricot, yellow, deep pink, and purple.

Sweet Pea

Tuberose

Sunflower

The head of the sunflower follows the sun as it moves across the sky, a trait that undoubtedly inspired its meanings, "adoration" and "loyalty" (two qualities certain to make any marriage a success). Bold and flashy, with raylike petals and disk-shaped dark centers, the sunflower is most at home at informal weddings. It comes in warm colors, from golden yellow to a deep reddish brown. This North American native is useful as well as beautiful: its seeds feed people and birds alike.

The sweet pea, which signifies "lasting pleasure," was first brought to England from Sicily in 1699, and the English have had a love affair with this delicate flower ever since. Its sweet scent and ruffled blossoms grown on a spindly green vine make this an old-fashioned favorite. Its many colors range from white to intense pinks and purples, and its scent can be strong and sweet.

Revel in the tuberose's Victorian meaning, "dangerous love or pleasures."

A native of Mexico, the tuberose has a very strong, heady scent, so small quantities of this flower go a long way. Its white, trumpet-shaped florets grow in clusters and open gradually along a light green stalk; the closed buds have a pink or green tinge. Most commonly used as a secondary flower, the tuberose lends bouquets a soft color along with its intoxicating fragrance.

The Tulip

The tulip was one of the most sought-after flowers in centuries past.

If you adore this springtime beauty, you're not alone. This Persian native first came to Europe in 1559 via Turkey, and, in an instance of foreign-language confusion the flower's name was derived from the Turkish word for turban. Although the flower is most often associated with the Netherlands, it wasn't, in fact, imported to this region until 1593, when it was met with unprecedented demand. The wealthy Europeans were particularly mad for the tulip, and newly cultivated varieties were named after rulers and noblemen; by the 1630s, "tulipomania" had swept across Europe. Thievery of coveted bulbs was common, and fortunes were won and lost in the bulb trade. Thankfully, today most tulips are nowhere near as costly and acquiring them isn't fraught with intrigue. Representing "consuming love" and "happy years," the tulip can be a meaningful wedding flower.

There are more than three thousand varieties of tulips, most with cup-shaped blossoms that sit atop thin stems with broad leaves. Tulips are grown in a huge range of colors, including white and cream; pastels like pink, yellow, and peach; and vibrant brights like magenta, red, and purple. Most tulips are unscented, although a few do have a mild, sweet fragrance. Available during much of the year, the most common tulips are quite affordable, while rarer varieties can be expensive. For weddings, tulips can enhance both elegant settings and more casual venues. They work well in almost any permutation, from bouquets to boutonnieres to table arrangements. Three main types are commonly used: Dutch, French, and parrot tulips.

Left: With their extra-long stems, French tulips are an elegant choice for a presentation bouquet, shown here with calla lilies.

1 Dutch Tulip

Widely available, this abundant flower shouldn't be overlooked just because it's common; its versatility and wide range of colors make it a useful flower for weddings. Typically seen at neighborhood florist shops, Dutch tulips have shorter stems and smaller blossoms than those of the French tulip.

2 Parrot Tulip

Also known as the Rembrandt or parakeet tulip, this showy sister is noted for its ruffled, striped petals in intense colors. Some varieties feature fringe-tipped petals for added drama. Although beautiful, their full, heavy heads tend to sag and droop and may cause stems to curve, which makes them somewhat unpredictable when used in arrangements.

3 French Tulip

Large, tapered heads spring from graceful stems in this elegant variety. The extra-long stems can be twelve inches or longer, which makes the French tulip a natural for presentation bouquets or tall centerpieces. More expensive than the Dutch variety, the French tulip is most often seen in cream, soft pink, and yellow pastels.

1   2

3

Tweedia

Best used as an accent flower, these cheery, star-shaped blossoms grow on climbing branches. While available in white and pink, tweedia is most admired in its unusual soft blue hue. A delicate tweedia boutonniere provides a little "something blue" for the groom's lapel.

Veronica

A natural for brides, veronica signifies "female fidelity."

Shaped like a plume, the tapered spike of veronica pokes out from the tops of arrangements and bouquets for a wild, garden-inspired look. Its white, pink, or blue color meshes with its greenery to provide a lush complement to more prominent varieties.

Zinnia

Brides seeking a spectrum of unforgettable color and a casual garden style will appreciate this perky, daisylike flower, which comes in hundreds of colors, including yellows, oranges, pinks, chartreuse, fuchsia, and lavender. The zinnia's meaning, "thoughts of friends," makes it an appropriate element in bridesmaid bouquets or reception centerpieces.

Beyond Flowers

In addition to flowers, berries and greenery can be used for a stunning effect. This unusual boutonniere mixes reddish hypericum berries with chartreuse lady's mantle, a popular greenery accent.

Think of the elements below as supporting players to the main stars of the show. Often used to flesh out arrangements and bouquets, they help complete the overall picture and keep flower costs down. Some of the elements can even be beautiful in their own right.

Greenery

Deep green or variegated leaves, whether from camellias, citrus trees, ivy, or host or galax plants, make a wonderful accent. Ferns and mosses can be used to add a woodland feel, and wintry evergreens can contribute fragrance. Grasses such as bear grass or wheat grass can add a sophisticated architectural structure to arrangements.

Natural Elements

Rugged plants like heather and thistle contribute an earthy texture and look, as can dried pods or sheaths of wheat. Miniature flowers such as baby's breath, lady's mantle, or Queen Anne's lace can add spots of frothy color. Berried branches, such as bittersweet, hypericum, and snowberry, also provide color and contrast, as can fruity varieties like branches of unripe blackberries or blueberries. Fruit or vegetable elements produces an effect reminiscent of classical still-life paintings.

Herbs

Valued since ancient times for their aromatic and medicinal qualities, fresh herbs add lushness and fragrance to an arrangement at a low cost. Lavender, eucalyptus, fennel, sage, mint, dill, and thyme are all possible options. Rosemary, in particular, has played a part in weddings throughout history; representing remembrance, it is often used to honor deceased loved ones.

Branches

Cuttings from blossoming cherry, apple, or dogwood trees have a springtime flair, as do fluffy pussy willows. Branches of preserved red and orange maple or oak leaves, complete with acorns, evoke autumn. Bamboo stalks or quince branches give an Asian look, while contorted willow branches or the pom-pom heads of viburnum cuttings add height and depth to arrangements.

ALSTROEMERIA
AMARYLLIS
ANEMONE
ASTER
BOUVARDIA
CALLA LILY
CAMELLIA
CARNATION
CHRYSANTHEMUM
DAFFODIL
DAISY
DELPHINIUM
FREESIA
GARDENIA
GLADIOLUS
GRAPE HYACINTH
HYACINTH
IRIS
LARKSPUR
LILAC
LILY
LILY OF THE VALLEY
LISIANTHUS
ORCHID
PEONY
PHLOX
RANUNCULUS
ROSE
SCABIOSA
STEPHANOTIS
STOCK
SWEET PEA
TUBEROSE
TULIP
VERONICA

Color Palettes

While an all-white bouquet is the most classic of wedding palettes, it certainly isn't the only option. Some brides choose to accent their white arrangement with a signature secondary color. Others depart from white entirely and opt for a colorful bouquet in pastels or brights, sometimes featuring their favorite hue or their wedding theme color. Whichever direction you choose to follow, it helps to know which flowers are available in which colors. On the next few pages, we'll walk you through the full floral color palette.

White

Innocence, purity, and newness—white symbolizes the start of a married couple's life together.

Along with the white gown and white cake, white flowers are a standard in Western weddings. Luckily, there are many varieties of white flowers, so traditional need not mean predictable. In fact, white can easily transform from casual to formal, and from classic to contemporary. This color can star on its own to create an elegant all-white wedding, or it can act in a supporting role as the perfect neutral complement to colored flowers. White has many incarnations—bright white, natural white, ivory, cream, alabaster, bone—and can be accented with hints of color, either in cool blues and greens or warmer yellows and pinks.

Left: You can't go wrong with an all-white bouquet. This example mixes lilacs, French and Dutch tulips, miniature calla lilies, and white roses.

Pink

Think pink. What do you envision—soft romanticism,
girlish prettiness, sultry sexuality?

Perhaps the most feminine of colors, pink can convey a range of emotions as wide
as its range of hues. In this palette you'll find the palest blush and the hottest
fuchsia, and in between a spectrum including powder puff, bubble gum, rose, and
magenta. Mix the more delicate pink shades with white or green, the stronger
tones with orange or red.

*Right: Did you ever think pink could be so many shades? This monochromatic
bouquet features hydrangeas, roses, and carnations in a range of pale to bright pink.*

ALSTROEMERIA
AMARYLLIS
ANEMONE
ASTER
BOUVARDIA
CALLA LILY
CAMELLIA
CARNATION
CORNFLOWER
COSMOS
DAHLIA
DELPHINIUM
FREESIA
GERBERA
GLADIOLUS
HYACINTH
HYDRANGEA
LARKSPUR
LILAC
LILY
LILY OF THE VALLEY
LISIANTHUS
ORCHID
PEONY
PHLOX
RANUNCULUS
ROSE
SCABIOSA
STOCK
SWEET PEA
TULIP
VERONICA
ZINNIA

ALSTROEMERIA
AMARYLLIS
ANEMONE
BOUVARDIA
CALLA LILY
CAMELLIA
CARNATION
DAFFODIL
DAHLIA
FREESIA
GERBERA
GLADIOLUS
LILY
ORCHID
RANUNCULUS
ROSE
SUNFLOWER
TULIP
ZINNIA

Red and Orange

Flowers in this fiery family can communicate many things, including heat, joy, passion, and love.

Brides choosing these vibrant hues are not afraid to let their true colors—or feelings—show. While the red rose may be the flower most commonly chosen from this palette, you'll find many varieties of flowers in a range of orange and red hues including peach, apricot, coral, russet, scarlet, ruby, burgundy. True orange has a tropical, summery exuberance, while its richer, more burnished tones are a natural for autumn affairs. Reds are a year-round favorite, taking on special significance around holidays like Valentine's Day and Christmas.

Left: Adventurous, attention-getting color is the signature of the orange and red palette. This bouquet features miniature red amaryllises, russet calla lilies, and bronze bicolor 'Leonidas' roses.

ANEMONE
ASTER
CALLA LILY
CORNFLOWER
DAHLIA
DELPHINIUM
FREESIA
GLADIOLUS
GRAPE HYACINTH
HYACINTH
HYDRANGEA
IRIS
LARKSPUR
LILAC
LISIANTHUS
ORCHID
PHLOX
ROSE
SCABIOSA
STOCK
SWEET PEA
TULIP
TWEEDIA
VERONICA

Blue and Purple

Looking for something special? True blues and regal purples might be the most rare colors in the world of flowers.

Purple, a symbolic color of royalty, makes a memorable floral statement. Its cohorts lavender, lilac, and mauve provide a softer look in this family of cool colors. And while it may be hard to believe, flowers *are* grown in blue—from pale and pastel tones to intense azure and violet shades. Colors in this palette are lovely when used monochromatically but are also beautiful when complemented by whites and creams, pinks and greens.

Right: Here, a bouquet contains purple veronicas, sapphire-colored hydrangeas, and delicate light-blue tweedias.

ALLIUM
ALSTROEMERIA
AMARYLLIS
CALLA LILY
CARNATION
CHRYSANTHEMUM
DAFFODIL
DAHLIA
FREESIA
GERBERA
GLADIOLUS
HYDRANGEA
IRIS
LILY
ORCHID
RANUNCULUS
ROSE
STOCK
SUNFLOWER
TULIP
ZINNIA

Yellow and Green

From soft butter to sunny lemon to glorious gold,
yellow can be undeniably rich.

Yellows blend beautifully with members of the white family, and they make a striking combination when mixed with cooler blues and purples. Green, a relative of yellow, has a new-life freshness that is soothing and tranquil. And if you thought that green only appeared on leaves and foliage, you may be surprised at the many flowers that come in extraordinary shades of emerald, grass, lime, and chartreuse. Green is an excellent complement to white, purple, and other colors.

Left: Fresh green signifies a new start. This bouquet is a mix of chartreuse cymbidium orchids, button mums, and lady's mantle, plus white-and-green parrot tulips and yellow-green roses.

2 GETTING STARTED

PRACTICAL CONSIDERATIONS

STYLE CONSIDERATIONS

FINDING A FLORIST

DOING IT YOURSELF

WEDDING FLOWER TIMELINE

WEDDING FLOWER WORKSHEET

Left: Before you meet with your florist, think about the feeling you want your flowers to communicate and come up with a vocabulary that conveys this feeling. Words like "hot, "bold," or "tropical" may result in a bouquet like this one made of gloriosa lilies and 'Splendid Renata' roses.

Now that you know your lilacs from your lilies, it's time to get down to the business of planning your wedding flowers. You'll be determining your wedding flower wants and needs and then taking the first steps toward making them a reality. In order to move ahead at this stage, you'll need to know your wedding budget, site, and date. You'll also need to have a sense of what you, your future spouse, and your team of attendants will be wearing, since all of these factors have a lot of bearing on your flower choices.

First, you'll explore the practical considerations, such as whether the wedding will be held indoors or out, and then you'll need to perform a little self-analysis to identify your floral style. Next, it will be time to decide who is going to create your flower arrangements: many brides choose to hire a professional florist, while others enlist the aid of friends and family or even opt to create their wedding flowers themselves. If you are in the first group, we'll prepare you to search for just the right florist. If you are in the second group, we'll provide basic do-it-yourself tricks to help you handle the job as smoothly as possible. At the end of this chapter, you'll find a checklist showing what you need to do when, followed by a worksheet to help you figure out your potential floral needs.

Practical Considerations

Before you decide which flowers will make up your bouquet or decorate your reception space, you will need to assess some practical matters. Certain factors—the formality of the event, the venue, the season and expected weather, your gown, and your budget—will play a major role in your choice of flower varieties, colors, and quantities. Weddings are like a symphony—all of the parts need to be in tune and play in harmony to produce a work of magic.

The Formality of Your Wedding

Certain rules of etiquette are as old as the day is long, and while you may want to buck some traditions, some are actually best to follow. The level of formality of your wedding, whether white tie, black tie, semiformal, or casual, should set the standard for your entire affair, including the flowers. For example, if you're having a black-tie affair in a gilded ballroom, consider classic blooms like roses, lilies, calla lilies, or orchids, possibly in an all-white palette. If your wedding will be a semiformal, suit-and-tie affair, elegant but not quite black tie, you may want to choose soft or bright colors in more unconventional varieties such as ranunculuses, hydrangeas, tulips, or amaryllises. Informal occasions offer a wide variety of alternatives. If you're getting hitched in your parents' backyard or barefoot on the beach, choose flowers with a freer, more casual feeling, such as gerberas, dahlias, cosmos, or sunflowers.

Your Site

Think about what your wedding site looks like. Do you want to highlight its good looks or transform it completely? A crystal-bedecked ballroom may call for just a few tasteful floral accents, but you may find that more flowers are necessary to jazz up an empty hall or restaurant banquet room. Will your site be filled to capacity with your guests, or will you need to compensate for extra space with additional decor? Flowers can be used to fill empty corners of an oversized space, but they should be scaled down if your site will be overflowing with guests. Is your venue built or decorated in a particular architectural style, say Art Deco or

Right: A demure nosegay combining white roses and gardenias pops with the presence of spiky blue thistle and vivid green lady's mantle.

English Tudor? Think about which flowers might fit the existing look of your site; calla lilies and roses, respectively, would be appropriate with these particular styles. Will your wedding be held outdoors? Perhaps the beauty of the surroundings will be enough to set the right mood, making additional flowers unnecessary. Whatever flowers you choose, try to pick varieties that complement the site and mood of your wedding.

The Season and Weather

The climate and time of year of your wedding will also influence your flower choices. First, you'll need to understand which varieties will be in season. Keeping in season will make it more likely that your flowers will endure throughout the day, and it will help you stick to your budget. Flowers look more festive and natural in their appropriate seasonal setting—tulips and hyacinths in spring, or dahlias and chrysanthemums in autumn, for instance. Flowers will be both fresher and less expensive during the seasons in which they are most commonly available. For example, while you might be able to get your hands on lilies of the valley during other parts of the year, you could end up paying three times as much as you would during spring, this flower's proper season. Now, consider the effects of temperature on your flowers. If you expect extreme heat or cold on your day, be sure to choose varieties that perform well under those conditions, to avoid drooping flower heads and excessive wilting. Once you've established how your wedding setting and season will affect your flower choices, move on to the more personal factors, such as your gown and budget.

Your Gown

All eyes will be on you as you walk down the aisle, so be sure that the blooms in your bouquet complement your gown. Think about the look of your gown, and its level of formality or informality. Like your reception site, your gown will affect your choice of flowers. A ball gown falls in the same formal category as the crystal-filled ballroom, while a slinky slip dress may fall in the same category as an on-the-beach wedding. Also, evaluate any special design details of your gown. For example, if the bodice is embroidered with daisies, you may want to consider selecting the same flowers for your bouquet. A gown heavily encrusted with pearls and beading might require simple blooms, while a minimalist gown design would allow for flowers that are more daring. You'll find more advice on the flowers in your bouquet in chapter 3.

A Word about Cost

The cost of flowers is an inexact science. A flower's price depends on many things. A particular variety or color may be very rare or difficult to grow. A flower may be transported over long distances and require special packaging and refrigeration, all of which add to its cost. Weather conditions in other parts of the world can wipe out a crop or disrupt air travel, making a relatively common flower suddenly more costly and difficult to find. And flower-intensive holidays, such as Valentine's Day or Mother's Day, inflate demand.

A Basic Spending Guide

So how are you going to spend your flower funds? Here's a rough guide, for a wedding with 10 members in the bridal party and 150 guests:

- Bridal bouquet, 7%
- Maid of honor and bridesmaid bouquets, 14%
- Boutonnieres for the groom, best man, ushers, fathers, and grandfathers, 5%
- Corsages for mothers and grandmothers, 5%
- Flower girl's basket, 1%
- Ceremony decorations, 12%
- Reception table centerpieces, 40%
- Other reception decorations, 15%
- Tossing bouquet, 1%

Say it with ... Silk?

We'd like to include a word or two here about faux flowers. Great strides have been made in the world of silk flower production, and types and prices are available to suit many styles and budgets. Why use silk flowers? They are relatively easy to get and can be a good option if you are looking to match a very specific color. Obviously, they do not perish; a bouquet made of silk flowers is a lasting keepsake. Silk flowers *can be* an economical choice, although some handmade or particularly lifelike varieties can cost just as much or even more than the real thing! If you are creating your bouquets and arrangements yourself, silk flowers can be a real time-saver, since they can be worked with at any time and don't require processing, refrigeration, or water. Brides who choose to use silk flowers may mix a few in with actual flowers, or they may even toss out the notion of real flowers completely and use only silk. It's a matter of personal choice.

Your Budget

For some brides, money is no object. For others, the budget is more of a concern and needs to be established up front. Be prepared to spend about 8 to 10 percent of your total wedding budget on your flowers. This amount will obviously differ from one wedding to another. For example, if your guests aren't big drinkers, axe the top-shelf liquor and go for gardenias in every centerpiece. Or, if you plan on the sounds of a DJ instead of a band, put the difference toward those rare garden roses you're dying to have. Regardless of how much you have to spend, your flowers will be beautiful if you choose them wisely. Here are some ways to save:

- Stay within season. The surest way to save money on your flowers is to stick with in-season varieties that don't need to be flown in from the other side of the globe. And here's a bonus: locally grown, seasonal options will be even more affordable, and their shorter transport time ensures freshness.
- Use special blooms sparingly. If you absolutely cannot live without a particular expensive variety, there is hope. While you may not be able to use this favored flower in mass quantities, you can use it in moderation, reserving it for special elements like your bouquet or your groom's boutonniere.
- Use inexpensive flowers in creative ways. A bouquet made entirely of massed baby's breath, carnations, or alstroemeria can be striking and affordable.
- Try stand-ins and supplements. If roses are beyond your budget, try their less expensive look-alike, lisianthus. Instead of going with costly single-variety bouquets and arrangements, consider adding more affordable flowers and greenery to flesh them out. Ivy, berries, and herbs are all economical and attractive additions.
- Downsize. Smaller bouquets and arrangements can be just as beautiful as large ones. Use only enough to set the scene. Let the bridesmaids carry a single dramatic flower down the aisle, or alternate high and low centerpieces on the reception tables to create an interesting visual effect and trim your costs significantly (but only employ this style if you have fifteen or more tables; any fewer and it might look awkward, not awesome).
- Recycle. One cost-efficient strategy is to reuse your ceremony decorations at your reception, if there is enough time between both events for transportation and setup. Depending on their size, altar arrangements can work beautifully at the reception entrance or even on the head table, and pew decorations can be used to decorate doors, bars, and food stations. If you are using the services of a florist, he or she may be able to handle transporting and setting up the arrangements. If you've created your flowers on your own, you'll need to enlist responsible friends to perform this task for you.

Style Considerations

National Flowers

ARGENTINA: Ceibo

AUSTRALIA: Golden Wattle

CHILE: Copihue

CHINA: Mudan (Tree Peony)

EGYPT: Lotus

ENGLAND: Red Rose

FINLAND: Lily of the Valley

FRANCE: Lily

INDIA: Lotus

NETHERLANDS: Tulip

PHILIPPINES: Sampaguita

PUERTO RICO: Puerto Rican Hibiscus

SOUTH AFRICA: Giant Protea

SWITZERLAND: Edelweiss

TAHITI: Tiare Tahiti

TURKEY: Tulip

UNITED STATES OF AMERICA: Rose

Left: The most personal bouquets include flowers with a significant meaning. This example is composed of four mini bouquets in a mix of flowers including 'Priscilla' gladiolous florets, orange tulips, orange protea, and burgundy dahlias bound together with dramatic fatsia japonica leaves and accented with eucalyptus buds. By using spiky protea, the bouquet gives a nod to the groom's South African background.

When it comes to personal style, who are you? Are you a neat freak who loves modern minimalist furniture? Or a country romantic who favors floral wallpaper and potpourri? Are a classic twin set and heels your signature, or do you prefer broken-in jeans and T-shirts? Think about what inspires you and what you want your wedding to say about you and your fiancé. These clues will help you draw a mental picture, even if it's a hazy one, of your wedding —and your wedding flowers.

Of course, many style decisions have already been made—you've picked your site, your season, and your gown, and your flowers will follow suit. But on the most basic level, your flower choices should come from what you like. Choose flowers that best fit your taste and personality and have meaning for you. Inevitably, breathtaking blooms will follow. Try the following approaches, to get yourself pointed in the right floral direction.

Signature Flower

One approach is to choose a main bloom and build around it. If you already have a favorite flower, your decision is easy. If you've been crazy about sunflowers since the age of five, of course you'll want to use them on your big day. If you don't have a favorite, get inspired by flipping through books and magazines. If a picture of peonies makes your heart skip a beat, use the picture as a guide. By all means, if you have a hankering for a particular flower, go with that—it's the best way to ensure you'll be delighted on your wedding day.

Favorite Color

If a specific flower doesn't jump out at you right away, try a specific hue. Start with a favorite shade or work within the color theme you may have already established for the wedding (such as the colors of your invitations or bridesmaids' dresses). Want to play it safe? You can't go wrong with all-white bouquets, the hallmark of wedding flowers. Feeling a little more daring? Pastels can work in almost any style of wedding. Or explore new and different color palettes—bright colors can create a festive, fun look, and deeper hues can create a lush richness.

Meaningful Flowers

Reflect on the people and events that have been meaningful to you. You might want to look to your family background, for example, and pay tribute to your Asian heritage with culturally significant blooms such as chrysanthemums or peonies. You can also honor your loved ones with your choice. If your mother carried stephanotis down the aisle, why not do the same? Perhaps your grandmother was fond of sweet peas—you can carry them in her honor. Maybe you're a Southern girl at heart—consider a bouquet of camellias or magnolias. Or maybe your fiancé thoughtfully showed up with orchids on your first date, and you can't imagine getting through your big day without them. Whatever you choose, you'll feel special carrying flowers that are meaningful to you.

Fragrance

Freesias, gardenias, hyacinths, lilacs, lilies, lilies of the valley, peonies, sweet peas, tuberoses, and, of course, roses, are all aromatic options. If you choose fragrant flowers, keep in mind any allergies you or members of your bridal party may have. Perhaps it sounds obvious, but this little detail is surprisingly often overlooked. If your maid of honor is shedding tears, you'll want to be sure they're due to joy, not to the flowers you selected. Also, if your wedding will be held outdoors, you may wish to steer clear of excessively fragrant blooms, which may attract pests of the stinging persuasion.

Wedding Theme

An overall theme can unify all your ideas and inspire your floral choices. Your theme might be based on an experience or common interest, like the semester you and your fiancé spent together in France or your shared love of the beach. Or you might plan your wedding around a season (such as spring or fall), a holiday (such as Christmas or the Fourth of July), or a setting (such as country charm or city sophistication). The flowers you select will bring your theme to life and give your wedding a unified feel.

Thinking through these key considerations is an essential step in your process of selecting wedding flowers. Now that you have an ideal floral paradise in mind, it's time to determine how to realize it.

Birth Month Flowers

JANUARY: Carnation

FEBRUARY: Violet

MARCH: Daffodil

APRIL: Sweet Pea

MAY: Lily of the Valley

JUNE: Rose

JULY: Larkspur

AUGUST: Gladiolus

SEPTEMBER: Aster

OCTOBER: Calendula

NOVEMBER: Chrysanthemum

DECEMBER: Narcissus

Finding a Florist

For many brides, finding the right florist is crucial. A florist is more than just someone who sells you roses—he or she is part visionary, part botanical guru. Your relationship with your florist is key. Of course, not all florists are the same. Some are "artists," who will take the lead from your cues and create something special just for you, and some are "craftspersons," who will listen to your vision and do their best to bring it to life. Neither is better or worse; your choice simply depends on how you want to participate in the process. So let's get you started finding the right florist for you.

The Prep

Begin researching your options about nine or ten months before your wedding, and plan to hire your professional (with a deposit and signed contract) at least six to eight months in advance. You might need to allow even more time if your chosen designer is popular, if you are getting married between June and October, or if your date is close to a holiday. Keep in mind that some sites only allow you to use certain florists. But if you are free to choose your own florist, you can start by inquiring among friends and family, who may have top-notch recommendations.

If you've attended a wedding where the flowers took your breath away, don't hesitate to call the bride and ask her whom she used. Pick the brain of your neighborhood florist, ask a bridal consultant, search the Web, or browse bridal magazines for florists in your area. Another smart option is to call your reception-site manager or concierge; frequently these professionals can suggest a floral designer who has worked in the space before and has a good sense of its dynamics. Other vendors can also be good sources of information. Your photographer and cake baker are visual people who might be able to clue you in to florists who could work with your style. Once you've finished sleuthing, you should have a list of florists' names and phone numbers to call.

The Pre-Interview

Ultimately, you will meet with the most promising prospects in person, but first you'll need to narrow down the pool with a preliminary phone interview. Start dialing, and ask each florist the following five questions. (It helps to keep a log of their answers.) If you're not satisfied with what a particular florist has to say or you feel your personalities just don't mesh, move on to the next one on your list.

The right florist is out there, and with a little persistence you'll find him or her. When your big day arrives, you'll be glad you put in a little extra effort.

1. *Is my wedding date available?*
   Obviously, if the answer is no, move on to the next florist on your list. If the answer is yes, continue asking questions.

2. *Do you charge a consultation fee?*
   The practice of charging a consultation fee is completely acceptable, and although most florists won't charge you for an initial meeting, some will. If they do, find out how much they charge. If you think the fee is too high, skip this florist and move on to the next.

3. *What is the average flower budget of the weddings you produce?*
   If the answer is twenty thousand dollars and you've only got five thousand, keep looking.

4. *What is your design style? Minimal? Traditional? Elegant? Edgy and modern?*
   Florists love explaining their artistic sensibilities–the styles they love, the flowers they favor, the palettes they adore. Consider whether the florist's views match your own ideas.

5. *How long have you been in business?*
   Certainly nothing is inherently wrong with a newer business, but the answer to this question will give you an idea of the number of events the florist may have handled before and his or her level of experience. If the florist has only been in business a short time, ask about his or her background so you can get an idea of his or her other relevant talents and experience—perhaps she's been a bridal gown designer or an artist.

The Consultation

Once you've found a few florists who sound like they have potential, the next step is to schedule consultations. The point of the consultation is to get to know the florist and their work, and to discuss your ideas and overall vision. Schedule consultations with at least two florists, even if you think you have already found the one for you; it helps to have a basis for comparison. Try to book your appointment during the florist's least-busy time (weekday mornings for most florists), so you're sure to get his or her utmost attention. Most important, be prepared to explain the details of your wedding and a sense of what you want. Bring anything that you think may prove helpful: magazine photos of flowers and arrangements, photos of other weddings, a list of your favorite flowers, pictures of your ceremony and reception sites, your worksheet of your anticipated floral needs (see pages 80–81). Be sure to bring pictures and swatches of your gown and your bridesmaids' dresses, so the designer can suggest complementary varieties and colors.

Cultural Connectivity

Looking to your heritage for inspiration? Go international with these floral traditions from the past and the present.

CHINA: As in the Victorian "language of flowers," meanings were attached to many flowers in the Chinese tradition. The gardenia represented feminine grace, the sunflower symbolized longevity, and peonies signified spring.

DENMARK AND SWEDEN: Grooms sewed small packets of strong-smelling herbs like garlic, chives, and rosemary into their clothes for good luck.

GREECE: Brides of ancient times often carried ivy at their weddings as a symbol of their never-ending love for their grooms, while their attendants wore hyacinth crowns.

INDIA: In some traditions, both the bride *and* the groom sported a floral headpiece. Additionally, the groom's brother sprinkled flower petals over the couple at the end of the ceremony to protect them from evil.

ITALY: According to custom, the front grill of the bridal getaway car is decorated with flowers, paving the road to a happy marriage.

JAPAN: In Japanese tradition, the camellia and the peony both stood for prosperity, while the chrysanthemum was revered as a noble flower.

THAILAND: The mothers of the bride and groom traditionally walked to the altar and draped *puang malai* (flower garlands) around the couple's shoulders to wish them good fortune in their life together.

At your meeting, tell the florist about your wedding—the location, date, time, formality, the number of attendants and guests, and your floral budget (don't be shy about divulging this last bit of information—a good florist will be able to work within *any* budget). Next, present the florist with the photos and sources of inspiration you've brought along, and start talking, using universal terms that your florist will understand—minimalist, elaborate, dramatic, subtle, colorful, monochromatic, traditional, natural. The better you communicate the look you're after, the better prepared your florist will be to create your vision. The key is to verbalize what you want, but also go in with an open mind.

During your consultation, be sure to get answers to these questions, then evaluate whether the florist is the one for you.

1. *Can you show me photographs of your work?*
   Some florists won't show examples of their work until a follow-up meeting. They should, however, have photographs of their recent work available.

2. *What flowers will be in season? Which varieties are best suited to my site? How can I maximize my options given the budget I have?*
   The answers are clues to a florist's expertise and will also give you a sense of what you can afford.

3. *What's the most innovative concept you've executed recently?*
   Decide if you are turned on—or off—by the response.

4. *Do you offer decorative items—vases, potted plants, arches, trellises, candelabra, urns? What do you charge for them?*
   Most florists will rent to you, but renting them yourself may be cheaper.

5. *Have you done weddings at my ceremony and/or reception sites before?*
   If so, he or she may have pictures of arrangements at your site and will know about what sizes, shapes, and colors work in the space.

6. *How big is your staff? Who will work on my wedding?*
   Make sure the designer you're interviewing will actually create the arrangements.

7. *How many weddings will you do the same day or weekend as ours?*
   The answer will tell you approximately how much time will be spent on you.

8. *Will you spend time at the site, setting up the arrangements and making sure everything is in order?*
   The answer will give you an idea of the level of service he or she provides. A full-service florist costs more, but you get what you pay for.

9. *Do you require a deposit? Is it refundable?*
   Some florists require an upfront fee to reserve your date. Before paying, be confident that this is the florist for you.

10. *Do you preserve bouquets?*
    Find out if the florist will do so, or refer to you to someone who does.

Now it's the florist's turn. Look at photos of weddings that the florist has worked on so you can see what he or she can really do. Be sure to point out what works for you and what doesn't, and which varieties and colors you absolutely must or *must not* have. Many florists say that hearing what you don't like is equally as helpful as determining what you do like. The florist should also show you samples of containers used for centerpieces, and the types of ribbon available for bouquets and corsages. (And be sure to check out the workspace—do you like what you see?)

Your florist will also ask you questions in order to get an idea of what flowers will work for you. He or she will ask you to describe the overall feeling of your wedding. He or she will also want to see photos of your dress, which may give further indication of your personal style or the mood that you want for your wedding.

Finally, assess whether you've arrived at a meeting of the minds. You'll be working with your florist for many months, so be sure that your personalities and styles mesh and that you trust this person to make your ideas and visions real. If at the end of your conversation you have a good feeling about the florist and his or her work, let the person know you'd like to work together, and ask him or her to put together a proposal. (Try to get proposals from at least two florists so you can compare them.)

The Proposal and Contract

When you give the florist the green light, he or she will draw up a proposal specifically outlining your floral needs as discussed at your consultation. The proposal should include an itemized list of the arrangements and services the florist would provide, the types of flowers he or she would use for each item, and the estimated total cost and rental fees. Review each proposal carefully, and compare them to see how they meet your needs and budget. Then make your decision.

Next, call the florist you have chosen and set up an appointment to review the proposal with him or her. During the review, make sure that you and the florist are in agreement on your vision and your budget. Clarify bouquet and arrangement styles, and the kinds of containers that will be used. Confirm the types of flowers you can expect to have on your wedding day (the florist should give you a range of varieties, since he or she will want to select the flowers that are at their peak at the time of your wedding). If necessary, revise the proposal, adjusting the number of bouquets, boutonnieres, corsages, and centerpieces, so you don't come up short at the last minute. Then sign the contract and submit a deposit.

Closer to your wedding date (about a month or two before), schedule a meeting with your florist to see actual samples of the bouquets and centerpieces for your wedding. If you don't like something about one of the pieces they've created for you, this is the time to speak up.

The Contract

Ready to sign? Read the contract and make sure it includes all of the items below. There's nothing worse than a binding contract that doesn't include all of the necessary fine print.

- Names, addresses, and telephone numbers for you and the vendor
- Date, times, and locations of your ceremony and reception
- Itemized list of all the flower arrangements you're buying, from bouquets to center-pieces, with exact names of varieties (if that's important to you), colors, and costs
- Flower alternatives (in your price range) to be used should a specific bloom be unavailable on your wedding day, plus unacceptable substitutions, if any
- List of items the florist will supply—centerpiece vases, trellises, or other accessories
- Florist's arrival times for setup at the ceremony and reception sites
- Time and location for delivery of bouquets and boutonnieres
- Name and mobile phone or pager number of the florist who will be on hand before and during the wedding
- Total cost and payment schedule
- Sales tax, rental fees, overtime charges, delivery fees, and setup fees
- Deposit amount and due date
- Balance amount and due date
- Cancellation/refund policy
- Florist's signature
- Your signature

Right: A little "something blue"—in this case, fragrant grape hyacinths—brightens a classic all-white bouquet of calla lilies and ranunculus.

Doing It Yourself

Left: Before you start arranging, lay out all your tools within easy reach: stem cutters, wire cutters, wire, floral tape, rubber bands, and so on. To strip a rose of its thorns or other flower of its greenery, hold the stem near the head with one hand and with the other place the stem stripper over the stem and pull down with one swift stroke.

If you (or your mother or one of your bridesmaids) have the time and possess some basic craft skills, you may want to make a simple bouquet, boutonniere, or centerpiece yourself. While these handcrafted items might not have the flawless look of those created by a professional, flowers that you have arranged yourself can still be beautiful. And, not only will you get to put your own personal stamp on your wedding, you might also save money. A word to the wise, however: If you plan to arrange your flowers yourself, it's best to stick to simple designs. Don't try for a lavish candelabra centerpiece or an overflowing cascading bouquet, both of which are best left to professionals. We've included basic instructions for creating a bouquet (see pages 98–99), a boutonniere (see pages 104–105), and a centerpiece (see pages 120–129). Consider this section an overview; we suggest that you consult one of the many available books on flower arranging for more in-depth tips and advice.

Before You Begin

First, make a list of the elements you'd like to create on your own. Boutonnieres, bouquets, and centerpieces are all items that you can create with relative ease. If you're feeling particularly ambitious, you might also attempt to arrange your own ceremony decorations, such as altar flowers and pew-end decorations, but these complicated arrangements are sometimes best left to the professionals.

Centerpieces can generally be made the day before the wedding, and bouquets and boutonnieres are best made the morning of the wedding. You may be preoccupied and busy the day before or the day of your wedding, but unfortunately you can't make these items much earlier; even if they're the picture of perfection a week ahead of time, obviously by the day of your wedding they won't be. If you aren't hiring a professional florist to produce your large-scale arrangements, consider using other, less perishable forms of decoration for your ceremony, such as candles, potted plants, and ribbons.

Making a Plan

While you may not be able to do the actual arranging very far in advance, you can certainly prepare for the task well ahead of time. Six to eight months before the wedding, set up a meeting with your mom, friends, bridesmaids, or anyone else who will be helping you with this project, so you can come up with a game plan and discuss responsibilities. Three to four months in advance, figure out how many flowers you'll need, plus any greenery, containers, and materials such as ribbon, floral wire, wire clippers, floral tape, OASIS floral foam, flower shears, buckets, boutonniere pins, and so on. Begin collecting the nonperishable materials. Call a florist to discuss the availability of flowers you'd like for your wedding and when to place an order. You can also start looking on-line for companies that sell flowers in "growers' bunches," packed and shipped to you directly from the growers. Plan to order about 10 to 20 percent more flowers than you think you'll really need, to accommodate for arranging mistakes, flowers that wilt, or stems that break. Choose a location where you will create your wedding flowers; be sure you have a work space big enough to hold a large table and a couple of trash cans (processing flowers creates a lot of debris).

The Trial Run

Don't wait until the week before your big day to take a stab at handcrafting your bouquets and arrangements. About two months in advance, do a trial run: put together trial versions of all the elements you plan on creating. Practice until you feel comfortable with your results. Be sure to keep track of how much time it takes you to make each one. About six weeks before your wedding, place the order for the flowers and set a date for the actual arranging with your team. A week or two before the flowers are due to arrive, call to confirm your order.

Final Preparations

Two to three days prior to your wedding, you can pick up your flowers and greenery (reserve the boxes the flowers come in so you can use them for transporting your arrangements later) and begin the process of conditioning the flowers—preparing the flowers to be arranged. You may need to recut stems, strip away leaves and thorns, and remove damaged petals. Different flower varieties have different conditioning needs, and with some varieties it may take a couple of days for the flower heads to open fully, so be sure to consult a flower-arranging book for specifics. Conditioning flowers can be dirty work; you'll want to wear gloves so you don't end up with *real* green thumbs on your wedding day. It is also a time-consuming and tiring activity, so be sure to schedule in some time to recuperate before your rehearsal dinner and wedding. You and your team will probably create your centerpieces the day before the ceremony, and your bouquet and your groom's boutonniere the morning of the ceremony.

Tricks of the Trade

You may not be a professional, but you can certainly employ the tricks the professionals use.

- Stick with hardy flowers, like hybrid tea roses, that can handle your poking and prodding. Also, ask the florist to order long-lasting flowers that will be delivered just before their peak. Certain flowers bought too far in advance or just beyond their peak might not make it through the wedding.

- Buy more flowers than you think you'll need; 10 to 20 percent more is a good amount. You may not get it exactly right on the first bouquet or two, and if a stem breaks or a head wilts you'll need some backup flowers.

- With many varieties, stems should be recut before the flowers are arranged (consult a flower-arranging book for specifics on your chosen varieties). Hold the stem ends underwater, and cut off about two inches at an angle. Immediately place stems in a bucket filled halfway with water and keep them there until you are ready to use them.

- While they are waiting to be arranged, the flowers should be nourished with cut-flower food (ask for this when you place your flower order).

- Be sure all your containers are scrupulously clean, and strip from the stem any leaves that fall below the water level, since they can rot if submerged, contributing to the decay of the flowers.

- After you arrange a bouquet in your hand, hold it together with a rubber band or floral tape and place the stem ends in water; you can add the finishing ribbon later.

Right: When making a dome-shaped bouquet or centerpiece, arrange the flowers one by one until you like the shape. Then hold the stems in place by wrapping them with floral tape or securing them with rubber bands.

Stem Treatments

The stems of a bouquet may be hidden in the shadows of the flowers above, but that doesn't mean they should be ignored. Here are some techniques that florists use.

BARE: This technique leaves much of the stem exposed with just a single piece of ribbon at the center. Bare stems work beautifully in a presentation bouquet and are a smart solution for DIY bouquets, because stems can be kept in water until the last minute. Good for semiformal or informal occasions.

WIRED: Florists use this technique to create a narrow handle when a bouquet has a lot of flowers and would otherwise be difficult to hold. The head of the flower is cut from the stem and attached to a wire. The wire stems are wrapped in floral tape or ribbon. Because of the time required, wired bouquets tend to come with a higher price tag. One flower that requires wiring, with no exception, is stephanotis, which has a soft stem.

WRAPPED: In this style, where the entire stem length of a bouquet is covered with ribbon, the type of ribbon is up to you: a casual wedding might call for playful gingham, but a black-tie affair might require simple satin.

Enlist a trusted friend or family member to transport your handcrafted arrangements to the site on the day of the wedding. To get the flowers ready to go, place crumpled tissue or newspaper in the boxes the flowers originally arrived in, to support the arrangements during transport. To prevent water spillage, don't completely fill the centerpiece vases with water or, depending on how far they need to be transported, leave them empty (be sure to delegate someone at the site to refill the vases when the centerpieces arrive). If your centerpieces are in glass containers, buffer them with newspaper, bubble wrap, or tissue so they don't come into contact with one another during their ride and break.

Wedding Flower Timeline

1 Year Before

- You're engaged? Congratulations! First, catch your breath. Then, dive in and set a date, create a budget (the floral portion is generally around 8 percent of your total), and start planning the guest list.
- Begin envisioning the style and location of your wedding—a formal hotel or a friend's loft? A backyard barbecue or an exotic beach?

9 to 11 Months Before

- Book your ceremony and reception site(s). Take note of whether the setting is formal or informal, indoors or out, decorative or plain.
- Start shopping for your gown.
- Consider developing a theme and a color scheme, and think about how to tie together all of your details—your venue, invitation, gown, bridesmaids' dresses, flowers, favors, and anything else.
- Get organized! Start a notebook to jot down your wedding ideas and a file folder to hold the pictures you'll tear out of magazines.
- Make a final decision on your gown. Is it formal? Informal? Elaborate? Simple? The style of your gown will inform your choice of bridal bouquet.
- Start researching flowers, and get a sense of the varieties that appeal to you.
- If you plan to hire a florist, start exploring the options in your area. To get recommendations, talk to recently married couples, the manager of your reception site, or your wedding consultant, if you've hired one.
- Narrow down your list of possible florists. Start making preliminary phone calls, asking the five pre-interview questions on page 70. Make a shortlist of the florists who sound like possibilities.

6 to 8 Months Before

- Choose your bridesmaids' dresses. Think about why you have chosen that particular color and style, since the look of their dresses will influence your choice of bridesmaids' bouquets.
- Take a tally of bridesmaids' bouquets, boutonnieres, and arrangements you will need (use the Wedding Flower Worksheet on pages 80–81 to help you).
- Set up initial consultations with the florists on your shortlist. Prep yourself for the consultation with our Consultation Questions on page 70. Collect proposals.
- Review the proposals your prospective florists have submitted, and choose the best option. Hold a follow-up meeting or phone call to go over and adjust the proposal, sign the florist's contract, and put down a deposit. (Don't miss our important contract points on page 71.)
- If you plan to do your own flowers, determine whose aid you might be able to enlist (mother, sister, aunt, bridesmaids, or anybody with a green thumb or a talent for crafts). Schedule a meeting to discuss ideas and needs, and set up a plan of attack.

Timing, they say, is everything.
Here's a play-by-play to help you stay on floral course.

2 to 3 Months Before

- If you'll be arranging your flowers yourself, assess the quantities of blooms, greenery, containers, and materials that you'll need. Research growers' bunches that can be purchased on-line; call a florist to discuss the availability of flowers you'd like for your wedding and find out when to place your order. Confirm the team of helpers who will be joining you on this project.
- Whether you're working with a professional florist or doing your flowers yourself, schedule a trial run, so you can see samples of finished bouquets and centerpieces. There shouldn't be any surprises on your wedding day.
- Research and book a vendor to preserve your bouquet.

6 Weeks Before

- If you are working with a florist, reconfirm your choices before he or she places the order for your flowers (florists generally place the order about two weeks before a wedding). Also reconfirm the vase styles, ribbons, and any other materials they'll be using.
- If you will be arranging your own flowers, place your order, and set up a date with your team to create the arrangements.

3 to 4 Weeks Before

- Work out wedding-day timing and details—including delivery and distribution of centerpieces, bouquets, and other arrangements— and draw up a schedule to share with your bridal party, florist, helpers, and any other important persons.

1 Week Before

- Designate a person to meet, greet, and handle each vendor—including the florist—on the wedding day.
- Whether you're working with a florist or doing your own flowers, confirm that your flower order has been correctly placed and successfully filled. With a florist, review delivery times and addresses, and discuss any last-minute changes.

2 to 3 Days Before

- If you are doing your own flowers, pick up the flowers and greenery and begin conditioning the flowers, if necessary.
- Confirm the final total due to the florist. Write the check, and designate someone to give it to the florist.

The Day Before

- If you are doing your own flowers, start arranging centerpieces now and make boutonnieres and corsages.

See page 161 for a timeline for the day of the wedding.

Wedding Flower Worksheet

PERSONAL FLOWERS	NUMBER	FLOWER VARIETIES OR ARRANGEMENT STYLE

Bouquets

Bride	_____	_____
Maid (or Matron) of Honor	_____	_____
Bridesmaid(s)	_____	_____
Flower Girl(s)	_____	_____
Junior Bridesmaid(s)	_____	_____
Tossing Bouquet	_____	_____

Boutonnieres

Groom	_____	_____
Best Man	_____	_____
Groomsmen	_____	_____
Usher(s)	_____	_____
Father(s)	_____	_____
Stepfather(s)	_____	_____
Grandfather(s)	_____	_____
Other Key Men (special uncle, readers, et al.)	_____	_____

Corsages

Mother(s)	_____	_____
Stepmother(s)	_____	_____
Grandmother(s)	_____	_____
Other Special Women (godmother, soloist, et al.)	_____	_____

Hair Ornaments

Bride	_____	_____
Maid (or Matron) of Honor	_____	_____
Bridesmaids	_____	_____
Flower Girl(s)	_____	_____
Junior Bridesmaid(s)	_____	_____

While you may not find every item on this list essential,
you should be able to use it to help you tally up the items you do need.

PERSONAL FLOWERS	NUMBER	FLOWER VARIETIES OR ARRANGEMENT STYLE

Ceremony

Entrance Wreath	_____	_____
Railing Garlands	_____	_____
Pew Ends	_____	_____
Altar Arrangements	_____	_____
Huppah	_____	_____
Archway	_____	_____
Petals for Runner and		_____
Flower Girl (number of bags)	_____	_____
Departure Tossing Petals		_____
(number of bags)	_____	_____

Reception

Entryway Arrangements	_____	_____
Place-Card Table Arrangement	_____	_____
Head Table Arrangement	_____	_____
Centerpiece Arrangements	_____	_____
Railing Garlands	_____	_____
Buffet Table Decorations	_____	_____
Bar Decorations	_____	_____
Drink Garnishes	_____	_____
Bathroom Bud Vases	_____	_____
Tent Decor	_____	_____
Cake Table Decorations	_____	_____
Wedding Cake Decorations	_____	_____
Car Decorations	_____	_____

Other

_____	_____	_____
_____	_____	_____
_____	_____	_____
_____	_____	_____

3 BOUQUETS AND PERSONAL FLOWERS

THE BRIDAL BOUQUET

BOUQUET PORTRAITS

GLOSSARY OF BOUQUET SHAPES

THE BOUTONNIERE

BRIDESMAIDS' BOUQUET

FLOWER GIRLS' BLOOMS

CORSAGES

Left: It is customary for the groom's boutonniere to be made with some of the same flowers found in the bride's bouquet. Here, a traditional stephanotis boutonniere perfectly complements the stephanotis found in the bride's Biedermeier bouquet pictured on page 85.

Part accessory, part medium for self-expression, and part work of art, your bridal bouquet is the most special handful of flowers you will ever hold. And, like the gorgeous gal carrying it, your bouquet will be the center of attention. But while the bride's bouquet is the star of the floral show, it wouldn't be anywhere without its companion, the groom's boutonniere. These corresponding elements link your gown and his tux, marking the two of you as special people on a special day.

Flowers are also used to acknowledge the members of your bridal party, your parents, and other big-day VIPs. These individuals will honor you by taking part in your life-changing event; through a gift of gorgeous flowers you can honor them and show how much they and their participation mean to you. Personal flowers such as boutonnieres, bridesmaids' bouquets, flower girls' blooms, and corsages generally take their cue for style from the bridal bouquet. However, as you're making decisions, don't hesitate to solicit the recipient's opinions. You may not know that your husband-to-be would prefer an unadorned calla lily as his boutonniere or that your mom adores orchids. When selecting personal flowers, just make sure that, while each person's flowers may have their own unique flair, they all come together to form a unified style.

In this chapter we'll discuss your bouquet, your gown, and the flowers of your bridal party. For inspiration, we include a selection of bouquets brought to life in simple, romantic, and natural styles. And just as brides come in all shapes and sizes, so do bouquets. In our glossary you'll find all the possible bouquet types, from the diminutive nosegay to the commanding cascade, so you can identify the right one for you.

The Bridal Bouquet

Like other scene-setting elements of your wedding, such as your invitation, your bouquet gives an indication of the style of the celebration. Its blooms should be selected thoughtfully, and its style should echo your own while complementing that of your wedding. In particular, the bridal bouquet establishes the style of the rest of your wedding flowers. For example, your groom will most likely wear a boutonniere made from one of the flower varieties found in your bouquet, and while your bouquet will be grander than your maids', theirs will borrow from its shape, varieties, and palette.

Whether classic, playful, glamorous, or sophisticated, your bouquet can be as individual, and as beautiful, as you are. To create the best possible bouquet, you will need to make several choices. First, you'll be choosing flower varieties. Be sure to look for flowers that are long-lasting without water and somewhat durable—your bouquet will be in motion and handled throughout the day. Next, you'll be deciding on color. An all-white bouquet is the most traditional, but accents of color or all-color bouquets are also beautiful. Think about using flowers in the hue of your bridesmaids' dresses or in your wedding color, if you have one. Then you'll choose the bouquet's shape. Here you'll need to consider the formality of your wedding while also taking into account the look of your gown. Finally, you'll decide on the style of the bouquet. Go with the overall feel of your wedding, whether it will be traditional and elegant or casual and relaxed.

You, Your Gown, and Your Bouquet

Think of your bouquet just as you would your jewelry, your veil, and your bridal shoes. Each of these individual accessories may be stunning on its own, but in order to form a complete package they also need to work together. You wouldn't wear a pair of flip-flops with your ball gown, and neither would (or should) you carry a hand-tied bouquet of wildflowers with it. The style of your bouquet should blend seamlessly with the other elements of your wedding attire.

Another important factor to consider is your body type. Generally, voluptuous brides should go with bigger bouquets; small nosegays might seem out of proportion. And petite brides should pass on the grand bouquets, since their tiny figures might get lost behind the sea of flowers. Think, too, about the scale of your gown. Here's a common rule of thumb to follow: the bigger the

How to Hold Your Bouquet

Hold your bouquet too high and you'll obscure your dress; hold it too low and no one will see the gorgeous blossoms that you chose so carefully. Most likely, one or two people will escort you down the aisle, so practice linking arms with them while holding your bouquet, and check out your form in a mirror.

HAND-HELD BOUQUET: Let your wrists fall above your hipbones and use both hands to hold the stems of the bouquet in front of your belly button.

PRESENTATION BOUQUET: Simply rest the bouquet on the lower part of your arm. Be sure you don't hold it too closely, however, or you'll risk crushing or mangling it!

Right: A variation on the round style of bouquet, the Biedermeier is one of the most formal a bride can carry. This colorful version includes ivory and pale pink roses in its outer rings, then stephanotis, followed by darker pink roses and a bullseye center of white ranunculus topped with a single stephanotis.

dress, the bigger the bouquet. A ball gown may be able to stand up to an overflowing cascading bouquet while a simple sheath may not.

Remember also that there may be embellishment or decoration on your gown that you don't want to hide from view. Rather than obscuring the beautiful beading or embroidery with a large cascading bouquet, consider carrying a presentation bouquet or a small nosegay.

Consider whether you'd like your hands to be free for the ceremony, and whether you'll be bothered by a larger bouquet, which by the end of the day can feel much heavier than it did in the beginning. And as you mull over your options, don't forget that while your wedding flowers are an important part of your bridal look, your guests will want to actually see you walking down the aisle, not just your bouquet.

How do you pull together a picture-perfect look? Below we've described the four most popular dress silhouettes and suggested bouquets to complement them.

Ball Gown: With its full skirt and fitted bodice, the ball gown begs for a bouquet that can match its stature. Don't miss out on your chance to carry a gorgeous cascading bouquet that spills over with flowers. If you'd prefer to focus on the dress, opt for a round bouquet, which can also hold its own but is simpler in style.

A-Line: Because of its clean, architectural structure, this style works on most bodies and also works with most bouquets. The nosegay and round bouquet are smart choices, since they perfectly complement the gown's neat lines and easy sophistication. A composite bouquet, resembling one giant blossom, is also a striking option.

Empire: Reminiscent of classical times, the Empire gown is defined by a horizontal seam under the bust. The longer skirt draws the eye downward and creates a long, lean look, so a hand-tied bouquet with long stems would mirror the dress's shape. A nosegay would be a subtle accent. For a period look, you could carry a tussy mussy.

Sheath: Long and lean or body-hugging and slinky, the sheath dress can be dressed up or down with flowers, depending on the formality of the wedding. A cascading bouquet works well with the dress's long lines. Or consider the presentation bouquet, which when held in the crook of the bride's arm breaks up the straight line of the dress but doesn't detract from her overall look.

The Prayer Book

Rather than carry a bouquet, some brides opt to carry a prayer book, either with blossoms decorating the cover, or with a stem placed between the pages, the blossom extending out of the top. If a bride's mother or grandmother carried a prayer book down the aisle, the bride might want to carry this family heirloom in her honor.

Left: A bouquet can help dress a gown up or down. Here, an A-line gown takes on a less formal feeling with a simple hand-tied bouquet of white roses, ranunculus, and anemones mixed with the soft texture of green lady's mantle.

1 2

3 4

Bouquet Portraits

To find the perfect bouquet for you, think of it in terms of an overall style such as simple, natural, or romantic. A simple bouquet, either in a traditional or modern sense, can work for just about any wedding style. Ideal for semi-formal or informal weddings, a natural bouquet is more freely styled and loosely arranged. A romantic bouquet is lush and overflowing, and can be tailored to many wedding styles. These styles, of course, are open to interpretation and adaptation. To help you identify your own style, browse the portraits on the following pages.

Simple

Simple can be classic or modern, slightly embellished with accent flowers, or clean and minimal.

A simple bouquet may let the bride's gown stand out, or it may capture the spotlight with its understated beauty. Picture a nosegay of mixed roses, an armload of calla lilies, a cluster of peonies tied with ribbon, a single gardenia, or a spray of orchids.

1 A simple bouquet may have only one variety of flower. A dainty posy of stephanotis, the most classic of wedding flowers, is subtle and elegant.

2 In a traditional sense, simple need not mean boring. This bouquet features roses in varying shades of whites and creams accented with pale yellow spray roses and lush white hydrangeas.

3 In a variation of the simple bouquet, a larger variety is the focal point while a smaller secondary flower provides an accent. These large heads of creamy French tulips are offset by tiny blossoms of narcissus and a collar of scented geranium leaves.

4 A bare-stemmed bouquet featuring a single graphic flower, like these calla lilies, is a striking modern choice. A note on stems: if you are storing your bouquet in water before the ceremony, don't forget to thoroughly blot the stems dry with a towel so as not to drip water on your dress.

Natural

Possessing a "just picked" look, the natural bouquet
seems to come straight from the garden.

Loosely arranged and simply tied with ribbon, the natural bouquet can include
backyard charmers like zinnia, cosmos, or sunflowers. Fragrant herbs can be
mixed in, along with all manner of greenery, grasses, pods, and blooms with a
wildflower look.

1   A natural bouquet can incorporate many textures. Here, white ranunculus
and blue tweedia are interspersed with thistle, lavender, oregano, and soft leaves
of lambs' ear.

2   While often passed over or used as filler, baby's breath takes on a surprising
modernity in an enormous mass. Bonus: This is also a very inexpensive bouquet.

3   This composition uses casual flowers in a formal shape: pee gee hydrangeas,
chamomile, Queen Anne's lace, lady's mantle, and tweedia. Mint adds greenery
and a subtle scent.

4   This early-autumn bouquet looks picked from the garden. Blossoms like
yellow and chocolate sunflowers mix with deep 'Black Magic' roses while orange
dahlias pull it all together. Using seasonal flowers can help cut costs.

1 2

3 4

1   2

3   4

Romantic

In a romantic bouquet, feminine, fragrant flowers are at their best.

Think of a cascading bouquet with a mix of bold blooms, or succumb to total girlishness with ruffle-petaled flowers like the carnation, parrot tulip, and frilly sweet pea. In a romantic bouquet, flowers can be complemented by luscious berry accents, swirling tendrils of ivy or other greenery, and ribbon.

1   For some, red equals romance, and this bouquet doesn't disappoint with its mix of vivid and deep red roses, red calla lilies, and—for a spicy finish—red peppers.

2   This armload of blooms features roses in a range of related hues—'Sahara', 'Rustique', and peach. Pee gee hydrangeas are a lovely accent to stock and pale blue tweedia.

3   Softly colored roses exude a romantic feeling. Here lavender roses mix with sweet peas and parrot tulips in the same palette. Sage-colored seeded eucalyptus keeps in the soft tones.

4   Trailing over a bride's arms, a cascade offers a visual impact of abundance. This example features purple lisianthus, deep burgundy peonies, dark purple calla lilies, red roses, and lavender passion flower.

Glossary of Bouquet Shapes

Posy

Nosegay

Before you began reading this book, you may have thought that the only difference between bouquets was the flowers in them; in fact, there are many different styles and shapes of bouquets. Some, such as the composite, are valued for their artistic flair; others, such as the cascade, are admired for their distinctive shape. Still others, such as the pomander, are chosen for the way in which they are carried. Read up on the different types of bouquets to find one that will work for you.

Smaller than a nosegay but similar in design, the posy is perfect for little hands, or for a bridesmaid's bouquet. Smaller blooms such as spray roses or grape hyacinths are ideal varieties. A few large-headed flowers, such as gardenias or peonies, can also make an impact. This simple posy features white ranunculuses in a collar of dark green leaves.

The small nosegay, approximately sixteen to eighteen inches in diameter, is a densely packed mound of flowers, greenery, and, occasionally, herbs. At once simple and elegant, the bouquet works best with compact blooms such as the rose, ranunculus, calla lily, and tulip. You can mix and match the flowers or use only one variety. Ideal for nearly every style of wedding, the nosegay can be dressed up or down, depending on your choice of flowers and stem treatments. Lush and full, this nosegay is designed with ranunculuses, roses, narcissi, hydrangeas, ornamental kale, china berries, and lady's mantle.

Round

Similar in style to a nosegay but generally larger, the classic round bouquet usually consists of large flowers that are loosely arranged. A round bouquet is a good option for the bride in a formal wedding who wants something bolder than a nosegay but less conspicuous than a cascading bouquet. This version includes tulips, narcissi, lilacs, hydrangeas, and seeded eucalyptus. The Biedermcier (see page 85), a variation of the round bouquet, consists of concentric circles of flowers, with one flower variety or one color per ring. The Biedermeier is best for formal or semiformal events.

Hand-Tied

This bouquet is a bunch of blooms that are wired together or casually hand-tied with ribbon. This bouquet works best in an informal wedding since it has a just-picked, natural look. Tie together a mix of summer garden flowers, or try French tulips for a simple yet elegant spring bouquet. This one features lisianthus flowers, lady's mantle, seeded eucalyptus, and astillbes.

Cascade

The cascade, or "shower," bouquet is the most formal and traditional of the bridal bouquets. Its waterfall-like spill of blooms is wired to "cascade" gracefully over the bride's hands. Petite brides should pass on this potentially overwhelming bouquet. Smaller blooms such as lilies of the valley, grape hyacinths, and lisianthus flowers are commonly used. Often, larger flowers such as lilies are used toward the top of the bouquet while other stems gracefully taper downward. The flowers can be accented with trailing English ivy or other greenery. This luxurious cascade is designed with a mix of ranunculuses, lady's mantle, amaryllises, hydrangeas, amaranth, astillbes, china berries, and ornamental cabbage.

Composite

Opposite: If none of the numerous
varieties of available flowers strike
your fancy, go for a composite
bouquet to make a clear statement of
individuality. An intricate creation,
individual petals from flowers such as
roses are wired together on a single
stem to create the illusion of a giant
flower. This composite bouquet joins
several amaryllis.

Pageant

Also known as a presentation bouquet,
this bunch of long-stemmed flowers
is cradled in the bride's arms—think
beauty-pageant winner. The best
flower choices for this bouquet have
long stems or branches, such as the
calla lily, lisianthus, delphinium,
French tulip, tuberose, and rose.
This traditional pageant bouquet
features roses.

Pomander

This small and compact bloom-covered
ball, about four to six inches in diameter,
is suspended from a ribbon worn
around the wrist—a good option if you
want your hands to be free. Roses are a
classic choice for decorating the ball.
Made with hydrangeas, this pomander
looks soft and full. A pomander is an
adorable alternative for your junior
bridesmaids and flower girls; just be
sure to take into account the age and
height of the child carrying it so it can
be sized accordingly.

Bridal Bouquet

You will need:

STEM STRIPPER

30 TO 60 STEMS OF A HARDY FLOWER
LIKE THE ROSE OR CARNATION
(20 TO 40 FOR EACH
BRIDESMAID BOUQUET)

BUCKET

STEM CUTTER OR VERY SHARP KNIFE

RUBBER BANDS OR FLORAL TAPE

PAPER TOWELS

RIBBON IN A COMPLEMENTARY
COLOR, 1 TO 2 INCHES WIDE

STRAIGHT PINS OR CORSAGE PINS

Be sure to stick to hardier flowers with big heads such as roses or carnations. Follow the same steps to make smaller versions for your bridesmaids; simply scale back the number of flowers. When the bouquet is complete, wrap the handle in ribbon in a coordinating color.

Plan to use thirty to sixty stems to make a bridal bouquet about eight inches in diameter. The bouquet takes about thirty to sixty minutes to construct. It is best to make the bouquet the morning of the wedding. Once the bouquet is constructed, keep the bare stems in water as long as you can and mist the heads well; then wrap the stems when you are ready.

First, process the flowers. Use your hands or a stem stripper to remove excess foliage and thorns, and pull off damaged or unattractive outer petals. Fill a sink or bucket with water, and holding the stems underwater use the stem cutter or knife to cut the stems at an angle about 2 inches from the bottom. Allow the flowers to drink for a few seconds with the stem ends underwater, then place the stems in a bucket filled halfway with cool water until you are ready to use them. If you are working with roses and the heads aren't open yet, you can force the blooms open by placing the stems in a bucket of hot water; only do this for a couple of minutes just before you are going to use the roses, otherwise you might kill them. Keep the stems long while you work with them; you'll trim them to a shorter length when you have finished constructing the bouquet.

1 Assemble the flowers. Take one stem at a time with one hand, and use your other hand to hold the flowers in place. Assemble four flowers at an even height in a square shape; these will be the ones at the center of the dome. Then arrange the other flowers one by one around the center flowers to create a dome shape. To better see what the bouquet will look like in your hand, stand in front of a mirror as you construct the bouquet to observe how the shape is progressing.

A simple single-flower bouquet in a classic domed shape complements most wedding gowns.

2 Secure the bouquet. Use a rubber band or floral tape to bind the stems at the spot where they naturally join (about 3 to 4 inches below the flower heads). Then repeat the binding toward the end of the stems, leaving about 2 inches of excess stem beneath the bind to trim later. At this point, you can either place the stems in water and wrap them later or continue to step 3.

3 Finish the handle. Cut the stem ends so they are all the same length, about 7 to 8 inches long. Dry off the stems with a paper towel. Cut a length of ribbon about three times as long as the length of the stems. Tuck the end of the ribbon inside the top bind and start wrapping in a spiral down the length of the stem. When you reach the bottom, wrap in a spiral back up the stem. At the top, tuck the cut end of the ribbon underneath and secure with a couple of pins pushed through the ribbon and into the stems. If you'd like a bow, cut a separate length of ribbon and tie it just beneath the flower heads.

4 The bouquet is finished. Wrap it in tissue and store it in the refrigerator until you are ready to leave for the ceremony.

The Boutonniere

Once worn daily as a signifier of a man's social status, the boutonniere, a flower traditionally worn in the buttonhole on the left lapel of a man's tuxedo or suit jacket, is now a special-occasion accent that hearkens back to the days when men and women dressed to the nines. The word *boutonniere* derives from the French word for buttonhole, specifically referring to the buttonhole on a man's lapel. The groom's boutonniere is distinct from those of his groomsmen. Generally, the elements used to make it are a reflection of some element in his bride's bouquet, either the color or the variety of flower. In a formal wedding where the bride carries a mix of roses, a coordinating rose boutonniere would be a perfect complement. An extremely formal white-tie affair would call for something classic and elegant, such as a floret of stephanotis or a miniature gardenia. On the informal front, a bride's daisy bouquet might inspire a boutonniere made of the same playful flower, to be worn on the groom's seersucker suit. Some couples even carry on the old-fashioned tradition of actually "plucking" the flower for the boutonniere from the bride's bouquet and pinning it on during the ceremony (although these days the boutonniere is actually premade and tucked into the bouquet for easy plucking and pinning during the ceremony).

Once you've chosen the groom's boutonniere, you'll need to make sure the other men in the wedding party look equally as sharp. Although they shouldn't match exactly, the boutonnieres of the groomsmen and ring bearer can be related to that of the groom, either in their color or flower variety. If the groom will wear a red rose, try giving his guys white ones. Or if he wears a brilliant blue grape hyacinth, let them complement the groom's boutonniere color by wearing blue hydrangeas. Keep in mind that the groomsmen's boutonnieres should also complement the bridesmaids' bouquets. Boutonnieres for fathers, stepfathers, grandfathers, readers, and other significant men need not relate to those of the groom and his groomsmen unless you prefer them to; a nice twist is to match the boutonnieres of these men with the corsages of their wives.

Regardless of who wears it or what it's made of, the boutonniere itself is always composed of the same few elements. At its heart is a central feature, which can be a single flower (such as a rose), a group of smaller flowers (such as lilies of the valley or stephanotis), or a non-floral element (such as a sprig of berries or an acorn). For an added flourish, a leaf, sprig of greenery, or a filler flower such as

Classic Boutonnieres

- A rosebud
- A gardenia
- A miniature calla lily
- A stephanotis floret
- A few stems of lily of the valley

Contemporary Boutonnieres

- An acorn and a leaf
- A tiny branch of berries
- Sprigs of dried lavender or fresh herbs
- A few hydrangea florets
- A head of grape hyacinths

Right: A rose boutonniere works for any wedding style. Here, a bed of fragrant rosemary and seeded eucalyptus adds color and texture.

1 2

3 4

How to Pin on a Boutonniere

In days past, the stem of a boutonniere flower was inserted through an actual buttonhole in a man's left lapel. Today, a lapel might have a faux buttonhole, or maybe none at all, so the boutonniere needs to be pinned.

1. Hold the boutonniere by the stem with your left hand; the flower should face away from the wearer.

2. Place the boutonniere on the wearer's left lapel, approximately four inches down from the tip of the left shoulder, either vertically or at a slight angle. Make sure that the flower is correctly positioned on the lapel before attempting to pin it.

3. Hold a pin with your right hand, and starting from behind the lapel, push it through the fabric just beneath the head of the flower.

4. Cross the length of the pin over the stem of the boutonniere, and reinsert the end into the fabric so the tip of the pin ends up behind the lapel. Be sure that the stem is held securely in place with the length of the pin holding it down.

baby's breath often backs the central element. The stems of all the components are bound together with ribbon or floral tape, and occasionally embellished with a bow. Generally speaking, the central element should be no larger than a medium-sized rose; anything bigger would be a distraction to the eye rather than an addition to the gentleman's polished look.

1   A few sprigs of pee gee hydrangea make for a lush boutonniere. This example works well with a natural-style bouquet like number 3 on page 91, or with a bouquet in a green palette like the orchid bouquet on page 32.

2   The deep hue of a 'Black Magic' rose contrasts dramatically with a bed of lady's mantle. Its dark red color would complement the bouquet of sunflowers and roses on page 91 or the bouquet of roses and red peppers on page 92.

3   For a rustic look, try using unripened berries for a boutonniere. The fruit theme can be carried through to other floral elements like the centerpieces (see a complementary still life example on the lower right corner of page 122).

4   A single white cymbidium orchid is a modern, minimalist take on the boutonniere. Its tropical feeling makes it a lovely accompaniment to a bouquet like the one on page 58.

Boutonniere

You will need:

STEM STRIPPER

A PERFECT, HARDY FLOWER LIKE
THE ROSE OR CARNATION

BUCKET

STEM CUTTER OR SHARP KNIFE

IVY LEAF, FERN FROND, OR OTHER
GREENERY

FLORAL WIRE

GREEN WAXED FLORAL TAPE

WIRE CUTTERS

PENCIL

RIBBON IN A COMPLEMENTARY
COLOR (OPTIONAL)

PEARL-TIPPED CORSAGE PINS

SEALABLE PLASTIC SANDWICH BAG

We suggest you use a hardy flower
with a big head such as a rose,
carnation, or miniature calla lily;
these flower are easy to work with
and can survive being handled. Plan
to have about three stems on hand
for each boutonniere to be sure you
have the perfect specimen and to

allow for mistakes. You might want
to practice first using one of the
other flowers. The boutonniere takes
about thirty to forty-five minutes
to construct. Boutonnieres can be
made the day before the wedding.

First, process the flowers. Use your
hands or a stem stripper to remove
excess foliage and thorns, and pull off
damaged or unattractive outer petals.
Fill a sink or bucket with water, and
holding the stems underwater use the
stem cutter or knife to cut the stems at
an angle about 2 inches from the
bottom. Allow the flowers to drink for
a few seconds with the stem ends
underwater, then place the stems in a
bucket filled halfway with cool water
until you are ready to use them. If you
are working with roses and the heads
aren't open yet, you can force the
blooms open by placing the stems in a
bucket of hot water; do this only for a
couple of minutes just before you are
going to use the roses, otherwise you
might kill them.

1 Choose a flower for the
boutonniere. Use a stem cutter or
sharp knife to cut the stem to a length
of approximately 3 inches. If there are
any leaves, you may wish to save them
to use as greenery. Next, create a
"bed" for the flower. Take an ivy leaf,
fern frond, or other bit of greenery and
place it behind the flower. The bed
should not extend much beyond the
top of the flower and should be visible
from the sides. Place a 6-inch piece of
wire behind the stems.

Making the boutonniere for your groom can be a fun and meaningful prewedding activity.

2 Prepare the stems. Starting from the top of the stems, begin to wrap floral tape down the stems in a spiral to secure them together; wrap until about three-quarters of an inch is covered. Then, trim away the excess stem and continue to wrap floral tape around the wire about 3 inches down, then wrap the tape back up toward the flower head. Once you're back at the top, wrap tape around several times to be sure it's secure. Trim the excess tape.

3 Finish the boutonniere stem. Trim the wired and wrapped stem so the total length is about 1 ½ inches. Then curl the end around a pencil point and pinch the tip to finish it. If you like, you can attach a ribbon bow. Depending on the weight of the boutonniere, insert one or two pearl-tipped pins into the stem to use later for attaching it to the lapel.

4 The boutonniere is finished. Mist it with water and place it in a sealable plastic sandwich bag (blow a puff of breath into the bag before you seal it to provide airspace around the boutonniere). You can place up to two boutonnieres in the same bag.

Bridesmaids' Bouquet

Your team of bridesmaids is made up of your best friends and loved ones, each of whom in some way symbolizes aspects of your passage through life. These women are a reflection of where you've been and the choices you've made while being there—in essence, they are a reflection of you. Choose your bridesmaids' bouquets in this spirit—they should reflect your own bouquet, either in color or shape, and come together to create a unified look.

Frequently, bridesmaids' bouquets are simpler, smaller versions of the bridal bouquet, especially in a formal wedding. For example, if you carry a round bouquet of roses, your maids might carry a smaller nosegay made of the same roses in the same colors. Bridesmaids might instead carry a scaled-down version of the bridal bouquet, but with different varieties of flowers from those carried by the bride, or with the same varieties in a different color.

Semiformal and informal affairs allow for a little more creativity; the bridesmaids' bouquets need not echo the shape of the bride's, and it is not even necessary for the bouquets to match one another. One option is to play with gradations of color, giving your maids bouquets of the same flower in related hues. For example, one bridesmaid could carry pale-pink peonies, a second bridesmaid could carry bright-pink peonies, and a third bridesmaid could carry magenta peonies. Or, consider a monochromatic look: one bridesmaid might carry purple sweet peas, a second might carry purple freesias, and a third might carry purple hyacinths. If you opt to give each maid a unique version of the bridesmaid bouquet, you may wish to unify the look with a matching ribbon.

At the most casual of weddings, many of the rules get tossed out altogether. While the bridesmaids' bouquets should still complement the bride's, how they do so is really up to you. Perhaps each maid could tote a unique bouquet, with each made of a different flower from your own bouquet, and even in a different color. Or you could have the bridesmaids express their own sense of style by carrying their favorite flower down the aisle, as long as it is in the same palette as yours.

Bouquet Embellishments

A bouquet need not only be composed of flowers. You can choose to embellish your bouquet or those of your bridesmaids with decorative elements to dress it up and personalize it. Here are a few elements you may consider using:

- feathers
- velvet millinery leaves
- wired crystals, pearls, or other gems
- beaded flowers
- buttons or silver charms

Right: Bridesmaids' dresses in dark tones are complemented by flowers in deep hues. Here, dark purple calla lilies play off pewter, with hand-beaded flowers and velvet leaves adding a sparkly formal effect.

1 2

3 4

The Tussy Mussy

A tussy mussy is the classic form of flower-based expression. Born in the Victorian age, this "talking bouquet" is a posy whose flowers carry a message in the language of flowers. The message itself is determined by the choice of flowers. Tussy mussies are anchored in elaborate silver cone-shaped holders.

For a by-the-book Victorian-style wedding, a tussy mussy, complete with holder, can add a quaint touch that shows that you've thought of every last detail. Or, if you want to send a message, you can profess your love for your sweetie using the flowers you select for this symbolic bouquet. If you'd prefer to carry a larger bouquet down the aisle but still love the idea of a tussy mussy, have your bridesmaids or flower girl carry them instead.

Your first step in your search for a tussy mussy holder may be to look among your family heirlooms. If either your mother or grandmother carried a tussy mussy as a bride, you might want to use her holder as your "something old." You may be able to find a holder through a florist; some holders are available on-line (www.theknot.com).

No matter which approach you take in choosing the bridesmaids' bouquets, do pay attention to the color of their dresses. Whether you're dressing your best pals in yellow taffeta or blue satin, make sure that the flowers they carry coordinate with the shade they're wearing. Once you've figured out what the bridesmaids will carry, you can move on to the flowers for the little ladies in your wedding.

1 A bridesmaid's dress in pale yellow is a good backdrop for flowers in a hot palette. Here, vivid orange and golden ranunculuses are accented with fragrant rosemary.

2 Sweet, girlish pastel dresses call for flowers in a similar spirit. A nosegay of lavender sweet peas and white lisianthus flowers is soft and pretty.

3 A few large flowers can be all you need to make a big impact. Huge pale-pink peonies with a collar of hosta leaves are a lovely complement to a pale sage bridesmaid's dress.

4 A striking single-flower bouquet is ideal for bridesmaids. This round bouquet of chartreuse cymbidium orchids really stands out against the color of the dress.

Flower Girls' Blooms

The concept of a young girl preceding a bride down the aisle is steeped in tradition, although what she tossed or carried has varied through the centuries. Ancient Greeks and Romans had their little ladies toss fertility-enhancing herbs and grains, while the girls in Elizabethan times carried nosegays. By Queen Victoria's reign, a flower girl toted a little floral hoop or the basket of petals we now know today.

Of course having a flower girl for your wedding isn't essential (some brides would rather not have any distractions on their big day), but if you choose to have one chances are she'll consider it the highlight of her young life. You can outfit this blushing beauty (or beauties—some brides opt for more than one) in any of several ways. You can grant her the traditional basket filled with petals (often from a type of flower in your own bouquet) to toss along the aisle. You can even cover the edges of the basket with heads of the same flower for a finishing touch. If you're worried about slipping on the petals when you make your entrance, have your girl carry a beautiful pomander on her wrist or wear a ring of vines and flowers on her arm or head. To ensure that your little lady completes her entrance without stopping in the aisle, ask her parents to position themselves toward the end of the aisle so she has a couple of friendly faces to aim for. Alternatively, if you'll have two flower girls, have them hold onto a garland of vines and flowers together; chances are, if one keeps walking, the others will follow suit!

Above: Don't forget flowers for your guests. If your place of worship doesn't allow your guests to throw rice (many do not since it is unhealthy for birds), inquire whether tossing rose petals is acceptable.

Right: A mix of rose petals is a classic choice for the flower girl to toss. Select colors to complement those of the flowers in the bridal bouquet.

Corsages

How to Pin On a Corsage

Even the most adept among us can be a bit perplexed when it's time to pin on a corsage. Here are some handy steps to commit to memory, so that no one gets accidentally pricked or has to forgo a flower because it won't stay attached.

1. Hold the corsage against the wearer's chest, just below the left shoulder. Be sure to take into account the neckline of the outfit and any jewelry when determining placement.

2. While holding the corsage in place, catch the fabric with the tip of the pin on one side of the stem near the base of the flower.

3. Guide the pin over, not through, the stem, at a slight downward angle, to help secure the corsage. Then catch the fabric with the pin on the other side of the stem to hold the corsage firmly in place, and push the tip of the pin out to the surface of the fabric. This will prevent the corsage from giving in to gravity and falling forward.

Left: Be sure to inquire what clothing the corsage recipient will be wearing so you can determine the appropriate blooms to select. This corsage is designed with ivory roses and tulips accented with seeded eucalyptus.

You're already aware of the important role your mom has played both in your life and in the planning of your wedding (occasional disagreements notwithstanding), so be sure to honor her—and your future mother-in-law—with beautiful corsages. And don't forget stepmothers, grandmothers, godmothers, readers, cantors, and any other special ladies. Giving them a corsage is a gracious way to let them know that you couldn't have gotten where you are without them, and that you value their participation in your wedding.

There are three main corsage designs, and each can serve a different purpose or play up a different style. The pinned-on corsage is placed on the left side of the bodice or lapel of the wearer's dress or suit, in the same position as a boutonniere. A wrist corsage is worn exactly where you would expect— secured on the wrist with an elastic band or pinned to the cuff of a sleeve. A third, increasingly popular option is a hand-held corsage, a small, simple posy similar to a bridesmaids' bouquet. As with boutonnieres, bigger is not necessarily better; corsages are accents used to enhance a look, not overpower it, so keep them simple: a single rose or orchid can be enough. Corsages really don't need to reflect the bridal bouquet or other wedding flowers; they simply need to fit the style of the wedding and the wearer. When selecting a corsage, you should consult the recipient to determine the style and fabric of the dress, suit, or blouse she will be wearing. A fancy wrist corsage may go wonderfully with your mother-in-law's strapless dress, while a pinned-on gardenia may be the perfect finishing touch for your grandmother's suit. Keep in mind that flimsy materials such as silk may sag under the weight of some pinned-on flowers, so if the lady in question will be wearing a silk dress you may want to opt for smaller, lighter-weight blooms or a wrist or hand-held corsage. For extra-special ladies, like your mom, you may wish to offer her a choice of blooms; she'll be thrilled to be included in the decision making, and she'll be touched that you considered her opinion.

4 CENTERPIECES AND DECORATIONS

THE CENTERPIECE

CENTERPIECE PORTRAITS

GLOSSARY OF CENTERPIECE
SHAPES AND STYLES

SCENE SETTERS

Left: The centerpiece is the star of the reception floral show, but you may also wish to greet each guest with a bloom of his or her own. Here, a centerpiece of abundant ruffled cattleya orchids, striped lady's slipper orchids, nerines, calla lilies, 'Bianca' roses, ballestri pods, and fuzzy lambs' tails is complemented by a fragrant gardenia at every place setting.

As your parents taught you, first impressions are important. When guests arrive for the ceremony, they'll notice the altar arrangements, *huppah,* or any other decorations. When they arrive at the reception, they'll be greeted with flowers at every turn, from the arrangement on the place-card table to the centerpieces on the dining tables. All of these elements, down to the last flower-filled bud vases in the bathrooms, help create a sense of place for your guests and evoke the mood or feeling of your wedding.

In this chapter, we focus on the centerpiece as the integral element of your floral decor. You'll see examples of centerpieces in simple, romantic, and natural styles, and you'll get to know your options in our centerpiece glossary. You can use our other ideas to help set the scene, too, from ceremony and reception decorations to floral accents for your cake and its table, plus flower-powered favors and other details.

Consider the mood you want to establish for your guests when they enter your ceremony and reception sites. Are you going for a modern vibe or a garden-heaven look? Is sophisticated elegance your goal, or are you after more of a funky, free-spirited atmosphere? Floral decor, from garland-wrapped classical columns to quirky garden-inspired topiary centerpieces, can transport guests to another world. Choose decorations that fit the space and its needs. Focus on the details that you love in the space (and the reasons you chose it) or, in some cases, those that you might need to hide. Know that you don't have to cover every surface with flowers; instead, you can strategically position decorations to create the feeling of an abundance of blooms. Then, once you've settled on the feeling you want to create, you can start to think about the individual elements that will help you achieve your goal.

The Centerpiece

Because your guests will be sitting at their tables during much of your reception (despite how hard you'll try to get them to dance), your centerpieces are one of the most crucial floral elements of your wedding. Not only should these arrangements express your wedding vision, they should tie together all of the other decorative elements in the reception. Where to begin? Start with the site itself. Consider the space and height of the room—soaring ceilings or intimate setting? This will help you determine the scale of the centerpieces. Tall arrangements are good space fillers, although they'll also put a dent in your budget. Professional florists recommend alternating high and low centerpieces in grand rooms, to help lower costs and make the space visually interesting. Next, think about your overall theme and how it might inform the style of the centerpieces; overflowing urns might be just the right touch for a Victorian look, while glass cubes of calla lilies might be more appropriate for a modern space. But don't limit yourself to flowers-only arrangements. Candles, whether low votives or tall tapers, can up the drama ante, while fruits and vegetables an evoke the spirit of the current season.

The most critical detail? The height of the centerpieces. Whether you choose a low globe arrangement or a tall candelabra style, be absolutely certain that your guests can actually *see* over or under the centerpieces; no guest wants to have to crane his neck all night in order to talk to those across from him. A good rule of thumb is to keep centerpieces under fourteen inches or over twenty inches high.

Centerpiece Games

After spending so much time (and money) on your centerpieces, you might not want to toss them in the garbage. The good news, there are some innovative means of distributing them. Before giving them away, make sure your florist isn't expecting the containers back.

- Donate the arrangements to a local hospital (call the hospital first to make sure they accept these kinds of donations).
- Play the birthday giveaway game—have your master of ceremonies announce that the person at each table whose birthday falls closest to your wedding date gets to take home the blossoms.
- Have your caterer tape a penny beneath one saucer at each table; whoever has the penny gets to take home the centerpiece.
- Using your guests' RSVP cards, hold a raffle, and draw cards to identify the lucky recipients.
- If you have breakaway centerpieces that can double as favors, place a note on the table or have your band leader invite guests to pick up a container as they leave.

Right: The centerpiece is the focal point of your reception tables. Here, a silver pedestal centerpiece at just the right height allows guests to converse. This full, dense arrangement features pink calla lilies, pink and yellow roses, burgundy orchids, and hydrangeas, pink begonias, and lady's mantle.

1

2

3

4

Centerpiece Portraits

In the same way you thought of overall styles for your bouquet, consider the same types—simple, natural, romantic—for your centerpieces. Think about the look you're trying to achieve with the flowers, as well as the container. The portraits on the next few pages should inspire you.

Simple

Whether you're shooting for classic elegance or modern minimalism, a simple centerpiece will fit the bill

Picture singular varieties or monochromatic colors arranged in unadorned geometric-shape containers—a glass globe filled with a dome of multicolored roses, a frosted cylinder brimming with pristine white calla lilies, a white porcelain cube packed with lush pink peonies, even a shallow bowl sprinkled with a trio of floating gardenias.

1 With just two colors, pink and green, this classic centerpiece offers simplicity in its palette. The domed arrangement includes a base of green hydrangea, a mix of pink spray roses with 'Sahara', 'Sudden Surprise', and 'Toscanini' rose varieties, pink ranunculus, and an airy accent of lady's mantle.

2 A single flower in quantity is a beautiful approach to a simple centerpiece. This low globe centerpiece features tropical white anthurium and accents of ornamental kale in a modern vase.

3 A modern approach to simple centerpiece uses multiples. Here, two parallel galvanized window boxes are filled with wheat grass, then three bunches of ornithogalum arabicum tied with leaves are placed in the grass. Plain square votives and silver holders mimic the trios and reinforce the theme.

4 A pedestal of roses gets a twist with seasonal grapes and pears. A common color palette ties it all together.

Romantic

The signature of a romantic centerpiece is abundance, so let your guests feast their eyes on a bountiful arrangement.

Look to ruffly flowers and ornate containers, still-life style and curling tendrils—a riot of colorful sweet peas in a cut-crystal vase, a cast-iron candelabra draped with ivy and roses, or a mound of lilacs with grapes spilling over the edges of a silver pedestal bowl.

1   A bright mix of color is offset in a Chinese porcelain container in this romantic arrangement of chartreuse cymbidium orchids, blue hydrangeas, blue delphiniums, grape hyacinths, pink alstroemerias, and 'Blue Curioso' roses.

2   Romantic takes a modern turn with this trio of arrangements in cast aluminum vases. One holds 'Polo' roses and peonies, another holds striped 'Hocus Pocus' roses, anemones, tuberoses, and stock, a third holds dark burgundy calla lilies and striped 'Hocus Pocus' roses.

3   Deep colors evoke a romantic richness. Here, burgundy peonies and dark wine-colored scabiosa mingle with a surprising addition—whole avocados as holders for the burgundy taper candles. A rusted container lends an antique look.

4   Composed of both flowers and fruit, a "still life" arrangement has a romantic, painterly feeling. This interpretation is arranged in an aged iron pedestal vase and features purple-green hydrangeas, burgundy anthuriums, burgundy and chartreuse orchids, red roses, and bells of Ireland with charming ladysmith apples. Dark red amaranth cascades over the edges of the vase.

1

2

3

4

1

2

3

4

Natural

Imagine garden flowers or wildflowers in unexpected containers—wispy cosmos in a galvanized bucket, cheeky sunflowers in an antique pitcher, chamomile and fresh herbs in a collection of mismatched teacups, or a mix of greens and grasses springing from a miniature wooden crate.

1   Non-floral elements like twigs are a natural addition to centerpieces. This striking winter arrangement features a core of red-stick dogwood surrounded by a ring of jewel-toned 'Royal Velvet' amaryllis and a halo of simple votives.

2   A textured container, like this stone urn, can help evoke a natural theme. This centerpiece has the look of being gathered by hand and includes 'Blue Curioso' roses, blue delphiniums, burgundy ranunculuses, tweedia, ornamental kale, lady's mantle, rosemary, and seeded eucalyptus.

3   In this centerpiece, a rustic bucket is overflowering with a mix of sunflowers accented with begonias, golden roses, orange tulips, burgundy orchids, orange spray roses, and lady's mantle.

4   Many natural elements converge in this striking centerpiece. Set in a carved block of ice, white cattleya orchids mingle with privet berries, desert pods, and an emu egg. As the ice melts, the elements settle and change their position. Amber-colored votives accent the brown colors of the different components.

Glossary of Centerpiece Shapes and Styles

Breakaway

Globe

At their most basic level, centerpieces are classified as "low" (under fourteen inches) or "high" (more than twenty inches). They come in many shapes and permutations. The style of a centerpiece is partially determined by the container in which it is arranged—picture how different a grouping of roses can look when arranged in a modern glass cube, as compared to a silver-footed vase.

Several small groupings of flowers in multiple individual containers are grouped to look like one big arrangement. The heights of the different containers are usually varied to create a more interesting visual effect, although the containers themselves generally resemble one another. Breakaway centerpieces are useful when you'd like guests to take the flowers home as favors: when the reception ends, guests can simply take a vase from their table.

These dome-shaped arrangements consist of glass bowls filled with flowers in a mounded design. The size of the bowl can vary, anywhere from about three inches to over a foot in diameter. Because they sit low on the table and are fairly economical, globe arrangements are popular.

Pedestal

Opposite: This style of arrangement often features cascading flowers and greenery. The container sits a few inches above the table on a little foot, and the bowl may be wide and low or tall and urn-shaped. Still-life tableaux in a mix of flowers and fruits are often created in this style.

Tiered

Opposite: This type of multilayered arrangement is sometimes placed in a vase that sits in the center of a low ring filled with complementary flowers. Because they are composed of many flowers and may require more than one container, tiered arrangements can be expensive.

Trumpet or Spray

The flared shape of this arrangement is due in part to the tall, trumpet-shaped vase that holds the flowers. Best for long-stemmed varieties such as lilies or French tulips.

Candelabra

This tall arrangement sits atop a metal stand and has four to six arms to hold taper candles. The flowers are placed in an attached or separate vase at the top of the stand and can be arranged in a cascading style or a tight mound.

DO IT YOURSELF

Centerpiece

You will need:

STEM STRIPPER

50 TO 75 STEMS OF A HARDY FLOWER
LIKE THE ROSE OR CARNATION

BUCKET

STEM CUTTER OR VERY SHARP KNIFE

GREEN ¼" ADHESIVE FLORAL TAPE

This classic centerpiece takes about thirty to sixty minutes to arrange. Hardy, large-headed flowers such as roses or carnations are best for this project. Depending on the size of your container, plan to use about fifty to seventy-five stems to make a centerpiece about ten inches in diameter. You can make the centerpieces the day before the wedding.

If you are using a clear vase, you can allow the stem ends to fan in the water for a modern look, or you can bind them for a more finished, clean appearance. Before you begin, have your containers ready and filled with clean water; you can add a drop of bleach or lemon-lime soda to the water to help prolong the life of the centerpiece.

First, process the flowers. Use your hands or a stem stripper to remove excess foliage and thorns, and pull off damaged or unattractive outer petals. Fill a sink or bucket with water, and holding the stems underwater use the stem cutter or knife to cut the stems at an angle about 2 inches from the bottom. Allow the flowers to drink for a few seconds with the stem ends underwater, then place the stems in a bucket filled halfway with cool water until you are ready to use them. If you are working with roses and the heads aren't open yet, you can force the blooms open by placing the stems in a bucket of hot water; do this only for a couple of minutes just before you are going to use the roses, otherwise you might kill them. Keep the stems long while you work with them; you'll trim them to a shorter length when you have finished arranging the centerpiece.

1 Assemble the flowers. Take one stem at a time with one hand, and use your other hand to hold the flowers in place. Assemble four flowers at an even height in a square shape; these will be the ones at the center of the arrangement. Then add the other flowers one by one around the center flowers to create a dome shape. As you're creating the dome, occasionally hold it up to your vase to gauge the width of the arrangement and adjust to create a pleasing overhang of the flowers over the edges.

A classic arrangement in a clear glass globe or cube is a lovely choice
that isn't too difficult to assemble yourself.

2 Secure the centerpiece. Use adhesive floral tape to bind the stems at the natural spot where they join (about 3 to 4 inches below the flower heads). If desired, repeat the binding toward the end of the stems, leaving about 2 inches excess beneath the bind to trim later.

3 Finish the centerpiece. Hold the arrangement alongside your container to gauge how much stem you'll need to trim from the ends. Trim the stems to the necessary length, cutting across on an angle to allow for better water absorption.

4 Gently place centerpiece arrangement into container. Once the centerpieces are completed, keep them misted and refrigerated or in a cool or air-conditioned room away from heat and light until you are ready to use them.

Scene Setters

What are scene setters, exactly? As the supporting players to the floral stars of your wedding, your bouquet and centerpieces, the scene setters are the additional floral elements that fill in the gaps and round out the spaces, both literally and figuratively, tying together theme ideas and completing your overall look. Do keep in mind that every one of these elements is not required. Rather, choose any or all according to your taste and budgetary constraints.

Altar Arrangement

Although you and your fiancé might provide enough scenery at the altar, an arrangement or two can give guests something else to gaze at. Because an altar arrangement is seen from a distance, it is usually composed of large-headed or long-stalked flowers, such as lilies, irises, larkspurs, delphiniums, or gladiolus, and complemented with greenery and filler. Of course, during the ceremony attention should remain on you, so the arrangement should be kept to one palette or similar tones—but feel free to choose a bright color, since churches and temples tend to be dimly lit. Be sure to check with the officiant at your house of worship to determine whether any floral restrictions are imposed; in addition, you may ask whether your church or temple already owns containers, like vases or urns, that you can use. If you're marrying on or near a religious holiday, the altar may already be decorated; ask your officiant what the decoration plans are around the time of your wedding. Some churches or synagogues expect you to leave the arrangement behind as a donation. So if you plan to move it to your reception site, ask first.

To ensure that the transfer of the altar flowers happens without a hitch, plan out the logistics of moving them beforehand. If your florist won't be on site (many will not stay through the ceremony), or if you've created your flower arrangements yourself, you'll need to designate a friend or family member to transport them. (One word to the wise: if an arrangement is extremely large, you may need to pay a florist or expert to carry it. No one will be happy if your aunt drops an unwieldy arrangement.)

Above: Garlands add greenery for a sense of continuity between the different decorative elements. Here, a smilax garland and stephanotis dress up a basket of programs.

Right: An arch can be used indoors or out to create a sense of architecture. This rustic wooden version is decorated with tendrils of smilax and ballestri pods accented with fragrant gardenias and stephanotis.

Left: Large-headed flowers in bright colors are perfectly fine for ceremony arrangements; since churches and temples tend to be dimly lit, these flowers will be easily visible to your guests. This arrangement coordinates with the arch and features pink peonies, roses, Dutch tulips, ballestri pods, amaranth, and privet berries.

Right: Decorating your chairs is a way to transform a standard rental item into something extraordinary. Here, smilax tendrils and stephanotis accent a banquet chair.

Pew-End Decorations

These little floral dandies can dress up your church or synagogue and lead the eye right to the altar. Before determining the sort of pew-end decorations you'll use, check with the officiant at your house of worship; many have rules regarding the method for their attachment, restricting the use of items such as nails, tacks, and tape. Place these decorations, which can be anything from matte ribbon bows to lengths of ivy to small baskets of blossoms, every two to three pews.

Chair Decorations

Decorating your reception or ceremony chairs is one way to transform a generic rented folding seat into something far from ordinary, and it can help to break up the space of a larger room. There are numerous ways to add a splash. Trim the backs with garlands of flowers that coordinate with the centerpieces, or attach a single flower or twist of ivy to the back of each chair. However, if you'd like to cover all of the chairs at the ceremony or reception with flowers, know that this will come at a cost. For a less costly option, decorate only the chairs at the end of each row or the head of each table. Or you can highlight your special spot for the day by decorating only your own nuptial chairs with something elegant, such as a floral monogram.

Wreaths and Garlands

Wreaths of flowers or greenery are the perfect way to set a celebratory mood right from the beginning. Since every guest will walk through the doorway of your ceremony and reception site, hang a wreath of your wedding flowers, anything from roses to daisies, to greet them and give them a taste of what's to come. Garlands are versatile decorations that can come in handy during both your ceremony and reception. These substantial ropelike vines are made from flower heads and greenery, such as evergreens, boxwood, and lemon leaves; they not only provide a lot of bang for your buck, they can also be used in countless ways. Wrap them around columns or railings, or drape them along the edges of the buffet tables or the bar. If you're having an outdoor ceremony, string garlands from chair to chair along the aisle, or wrap them around an arch.

Huppah and Canopy Decorations

Jewish brides and grooms traditionally marry underneath a *huppah,* or canopy, a symbol of the new home they will make together. This custom dates to the tent-dwelling nomadic days in the desert when all wedding ceremonies were held outdoors by necessity, and the huppah created an intimate, sacred space. If you're planning to marry underneath one, consider embellishing it with flowers. You can do this by simply winding ivy tendrils around the legs, creating a lavish canopy made of interwoven flowers, or anything in between. You can also drape a favorite or sentimental piece of fabric, like a prayer shawl or a blanket, over the top of the huppah, and add blossoms that complement your other ceremony flowers.

Arch Decorations

Crafted of greenery, flowers, or even fabric, arches can create a sense of architecture in a spot where there isn't any (such as outside), jazz up a plain interior, or accentuate an entryway (such as a church door or ballroom entrance). You may opt to place arches at either end of the ceremony aisle to create a designated starting or finishing point, so guests know where to look for your breathtaking entrance. If you're having an outdoor ceremony, consider building an arch from natural elements, such as branches, twigs, and vines.

Above: A little flower pot filled with irish moss or flowers serves not only as a place card but also as a favor for guests to take home.

Right: Welcome guests with a gorgeous arrangement as they find their seating assignments. This arrangement continues a green and white color palette with 'Casablanca' lilies, calla lilies, lisianthus flowers, blush-colored roses, veronicas, and seeded eucalyptus. A sprinkling of rose petals is the final detail.

Place-Card Table or Gift Table Arrangements

Your guests may be stopping to pick up their table assignment and leave your gift, so consider placing an arrangement at each of these spots to greet them. These arrangements may be similar to your altar arrangements in scope but smaller in scale, and they should reflect the color scheme of your centerpieces. In fact, these might *be* your altar arrangements, since you can trim your floral budget by reusing the ceremony flowers on these tables and in other spots at the reception. If you will be reusing these flowers, you'll want to be sure that they are designed to look beautiful in both settings.

Cake Decorations

Your cake is bound to be one of the most photographed items at your reception. Why not make it, and the table it stands on, utterly gorgeous? Flowers can serve as jewelry for your cake and can be used to dress it up to complement your other floral choices and the overall style of the event. An afternoon wedding in the country might call for a cake highlighted with daisies; an evening black-tie affair might be the perfect setting for a cake stacked with tiers of roses. Before you choose the specific blossoms for your cake, check with a florist to see which ones are edible or nonpoisonous. It is *absolutely essential* that you make sure that the flowers for your cake haven't been sprayed with insecticides or other such toxic materials. Flowers that often get the green light include roses, orchids, lilies, violets, and hydrangeas. If you'd rather pass on fresh blossoms, consider using sugared flowers, fresh blossoms or petals (most often roses) that have been coated in sugar.

How you go about decorating your cake is up to you and your cake designer. There are three basic decorating styles when it comes to using cake flowers: strewing them about the tiers, placing a cascading garland on the top and wrapping it around to the bottom, and creating actual tiers of flowers that alternate with tiers of cake. Flip through magazines, surf the Web, and check out your baker's portfolio to find the style and design that would best serve as the highlight of your wedding. If you are using the services of a florist, inquire whether he or she might be willing to contact your cake designer to determine which of them would be responsible for purchasing these flowers.

Whether or not your cake is decorated with flowers, your cake table certainly can be. You might want to place your bouquet on the cake table for the guests to admire. Or you might scatter petals or lay garlands or leaves around the base of the cake. You could also play up the theme of your wedding, perhaps surrounding your cake with maple leaves for an autumn look or creating a bed of orchids for a tropical atmosphere.

Above: A favor of bulbs or seeds is a memorable gift of flowers for your guests to take home.

Left: Don't stop at centerpieces for reception decorations—flowers make graceful accents for drinks, hors d'oeuvres, and salads, too. Just be sure your caterer uses edible flowers that haven't been treated with pesticides.

Don't stop at your cake when it comes to using edible flowers. Food and drink can be spiced with these glorious garnishes. Ask your caterer about topping salads or garnishing appetizers with edible flowers, such as nasturtiums and pansies. The cocktail hour will be an even bigger blast when you playfully put flowers into the mix. A tiny rosebud in a glass of champagne or a tropical drink garnished with an orchid is a delightful surprise.

Favors and Finishing Touches

Floral decor need not stop with centerpieces and arrangements; let blossoms accent every last finishing touch. Decorate place cards with dried petals or even a fresh flower; placing the cards on a bed of petals is a lovely way to present them to guests. Beautify napkins with an unexpected flower or sprig of herbs tucked into the folds. Treat guests to favors containing a packet of seeds or bulbs for the type of flowers you carried in your bouquet, accompanied by a small card with a message asking guests to plant them in honor of your marriage. Other wonderful floral favor ideas include miniature flowerpots, potted plants, or breakaway sections of your centerpiece. (If you've used the services of a florist to create a breakaway, just make sure he or she isn't expecting the vases or pots to be returned.)

Above: Even your cake can get in on the floral action. Talk to your baker and your florist about coordinating fresh flowers on your cake with those in your bouquet. Here, fresh tiers of pink roses, blue hydrangeas, and chartreuse lady's mantle alternate with layers of wedding cake.

Right: Lifelike gum-paste flowers are a more lasting alternative to the real thing. Made by hand, they are edible and also make lovely keepsakes. This classic tiered cake is decorated with gum-paste rosebuds and oriental lilies.

Patrick Mavros

5 PUTTING IT ALL TOGETHER

WEDDING PORTRAITS

THE BIG DAY

WEDDING DAY FLORAL TIMELINE

The wedding day is when your vision finally comes alive– bouquets, boutonnieres, centerpieces, table settings, and other decorations all working in harmony.

By this point, you're nearly an expert on the intricacies of wedding flowers. You've learned all about different blooms, found your favorites, assessed your style, contemplated the best bouquet, plotted out the personal flowers for your gang, and considered your centerpiece choices. Now, how do you pull it all together for your big day? In this chapter, we'll illustrate how these different components work with each other in four sample weddings.

Then, with your own wedding not too far off, you'll need to read up on all of the important big-day details. Since the best way to ensure smooth sailing is to stay organized, we've provided a timeline for your wedding. There will be bouquets to hand out, boutonnieres and corsages to pin on, and many other things to do. By considering all of the logistics well in advance, you'll be much more likely to preserve your sanity, stay calm, and pull off your wedding day without a hitch. But first, flowers for a simple spring wedding, a contemporary summer wedding, a natural fall wedding, and a romantic winter wedding.

Wedding Portraits

A Springtime Affair

As the cooler air of winter gives way to soft, welcoming breezes, spring reawakens our dormant senses.

Spring is the season of rebirth and renewal, and the world around us rouses from its hibernation to greet the warmer temperatures and melting snow. Lovely, fresh shades of green are everywhere, and flowers come alive in these sun-filled days, as blossoms, both in gardens and on trees, shrug off the winter frost and begin to bloom. If you're marrying during this glorious season you can take full advantage of nature spreading its wings, as seasonal bulbs, such as hyacinths, tulips, and daffodils, pop their heads up from the soil. With a wide variety of flowers and branches available during these months, you can truly give your wedding a garden-like feel and take inspiration in the soft seasonal pastels of pinks, yellows, and blues.

Right: Inspired by the palette and fragrance of spring flowers, Renny Reynolds created a table setting to suit the season. Bulb flowers play a prominent role throughout the centerpieces, bouquets, and decorations.

1

2

3

4

A Springtime Affair

1 The bride's cascade bouquet is a mix of fragrant flowers such as grape hyacinths, paper white narcissi, jonquils, lilies of the valley, and lavender sweet peas accented by pale yellow and apricot-colored ranunculuses and white calla lilies. Her groom's boutonniere is a classic: a white miniature calla lily on a bed of ivy leaves.

2 Embellished red fruit and floral china is set at every place, and each guest has his or her own little bunch of fragrant grape hyacinth. The blue-stemmed goblets accent the colors of the plaid organza tablecloth.

3 Special chairs for the bridal party are decorated with bunches of paperwhites tied with sheer yellow ribbon.

4 Arranged in charming French-wire baskets, the centerpieces have a colorful seasonal mix of blush pink peonies, dark pink calla lilies, lavender sweet peas, pale pink miniature ranunculuses, fragrant English garden roses, jonquils, and pink lisianthus flowers with a splash of green from scented geranium leaves and pom-poms of viburnum.

Gloria Paris

A Summer Celebration

Mother Nature is at her showiest, and almost anything goes. Think hot summer nights and tropical colors.

Summer is the season of playful exuberance. Everything, including the temperature, rises in intensity. Find inspiration in the sultry heat and full, lush flowering gardens, which are overflowing with hot pink, bright orange, and riotous red blossoms. Have a little fun and incorporate bright flowers at every turn. If you'll be a beachside bride, play up the gorgeous blues of the pool and ocean. Or, if you'd prefer to take a more understated route, start with a palette of white and add color from there.

Left: With a sophisticated city wedding in mind, florist Michael George took a cue from summer's heat with a palette of hot colors—magenta, lime, and orange. The minimalist style is still lush, with hundreds of orchids contributing to its bold design.

A Summer Celebration

1   This centerpiece is created using multiple clear glass containers that let the orange Vanda orchids, green dendrobium orchids, and pink orchids be the stars. The varied heights generate visual interest. Votives around the table softly highlight the color of the flowers.

2   Continuing the theme of orchids, the magnificent cattleya orchid in white is reserved for the bride's bouquet and the groom's boutonniere.

3   Chairs for the bride and groom are decorated with orchids to match the centerpieces and the bridesmaids' bouquets.

4   Each frosted-glass place setting is graced with a hybrid orchid featuring the pink and green colors of the centerpiece varieties.

1

2

3

4

An Autumn Event

In autumn, the temperature isn't the only thing changing; leaves take on glorious hues of red, copper, orange, and gold.

After the dog days of summer, the crisp fall breezes always feel like a literal breath of fresh air. The harvest of the season brings in homey bounty like pumpkins, squashes, and apples to mix in with your floral decor. Fall weddings take their style cues from the lush foliage colors, as autumn flowers, in colors ranging from gold to orange to purple, can be magnificent in their richness. Get in the mood and pin a maple leaf on the groom's lapel. For your own blooms, consider carrying gorgeous russet 'Leonidas' roses or copper-colored chrysanthemums.

Right: For a casual autumn wedding in the country, florist Saundra Parks made the most of the season's bounty and palette. Rich terra-cotta, russet, and orange hues mingle with rustic textures.

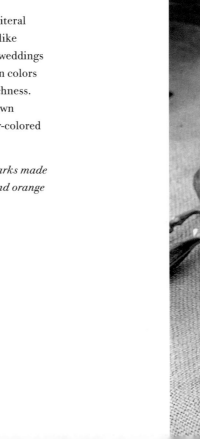

An Autumn Event

1   Chair backs are lushly adorned with a cone of berries called mungiot wrapped in cocoa fiber.

2   For the centerpiece, three related arrangements interact with pea-green tapers wrapped in cocoa fiber. The tallest arrangement features persimmons, mungiot, and malta balls; the medium arrangement builds on the theme with pink cockscomb flowers and orange ranunculuses; and the smallest is a miniature version of the middle size. Each is wrapped in ivy and has a base of moss.

3   Set on top of a burlap overlay, each place setting has a terra-cotta linen napkin simply wrapped with hypericum berries. Floral china and rustic wood-handled flatware complete the look.

4   Wrapped in a collar of cocoa fiber, the bride's bouquet recalls the look of the centerpieces and captures autumn's palette with persimmons, pink cockscomb flowers, and hypericum berries. The groom's boutonniere, a charming little bundle of hypericum berries, is wrapped with twigs.

Patrick Massens

A Winter Evening

Although most of nature is sleeping during this season, other elements are at their most beautiful

Winter brides know the hidden secrets of the season—the peaceful snowfalls, the shimmer of icy branches, the contrast of evergreens against the winter sky. Build a palette of whites, creams, and ivories, so that your entire reception venue resembles the view from the window, and add silver, gold, or crystal touches to give it that extra sparkle. Or take a different approach, and revel in the richness of glorious red hues and lush, overflowing arrangements. Some bulb flowers, such as hyacinth and amaryllis, can be tricked into appearing at this time of year. Or, bring the outside in. Take advantage of winter's evergreens, pines, and holly, and make the most of seasonal potted plants such as poinsettias and flowering cactuses for a colorful contrast. And over the holidays, don't forget your mistletoe. Hang it in doorways, archways, and anywhere else you think your guests (and you) should pucker up for a smooch.

Left: In contrast to a traditional white winter wedding, florist Preston Bailey reinterprets the best of the season with jewel-tone red hues and lush abundance for a formal affair. Fruits like grapes and apples lend a still life feeling, while surprising varieties of roses, amaryllises, and orchids create a colorful richness.

A Winter Evening

1 The impressive multilevel crystal candelabra overflows with color. On top is a luxurious ball of burgundy hydrangeas, pink peonies, burgundy cymbidium orchids, dark purple calla lilies, red amaryllises, amaranth, privet berries, and roses in 'Leonidas' (russet bicolor), 'Black Magic' (deep black-red), 'Cleopatra' (red-ivory bicolor), and 'Meicandi' (speckled pink) varieties. Bunches of dark purple grapes suspend seductively from the arms of the candelabra. Many of the same flowers encircle the base.

2 Each place setting is an elegant arrangement of etched silver chargers and goblets with a sprig of privet berries tucked into each hemstitched napkin. Votives in silver holders illuminate the base of the centerpiece, and dishes of floating composite flowers made from bicolor 'Cleopatra' roses provide a sumptuous finishing touch.

3 Color continues with the design of the personal flowers. The most colorful of the group, the bride's bouquet, is a gorgeous mix of burgundy calla lilies, coral nerines, red bruneas, and roses in extra-dark 'Black Magic' and 'Black Beauty' varieties. The bridesmaids' bouquets feature the rose in all its glory, including 'Leonidas', 'Black Tea', and 'Sacha' varieties accented with the soft pink of pepperberries.

4 Looking good enough to eat, an artistic arrangement of lady apples, grapes, plums, and peaches decorates the base of the candelabra.

1

2

3

4

The Big Day

After months of researching, planning, and dreaming, your wedding day is finally here. Amid all of the excitement, try to relax a bit. You've put in all the necessary work and preparation for your wedding day, and now is the time to see your vision fully realized. No more wondering if your arrangements are too tall; no more worrying that your great-grandma will crush her corsage from constantly hugging you. You'll finally get to carry your bouquet down the aisle and see your beautiful decorations fill your wedding space. This is your day, so why not enjoy it? Here are a few pointers to help make sure you do.

Red equals romance. In this stunning cascade bouquet, rich, voluptuous 'Red Lion' amaryllis, 'Fancy Amazon' roses, and china berries create a look that's red-hot.

Prewedding Preparation

Whether you have a morning, afternoon, or evening wedding, you'll need to be "florally organized" well in advance of the actual affair. Of course, each wedding is unique and that includes the scheduling that is involved. Whether you're using a florist or doing the flowers on your own, check with the appropriate people at both your reception and ceremony sites to determine when you can begin setting up and how long you'll have to do so. If you are working with a florist, be sure to discuss how they like to go about setting up. A florist with a larger staff may be able to work at the ceremony and reception sites simultaneously, while a smaller operation may need to work on one site first, then move on to the other. If you're doing the flowers on your own, make sure your team of helpers will have enough time to set up all of the decorations before the wedding.

The Arrival of Your Flowers

If you are working with a florist, you'll need to establish when and where your flowers will arrive, and how they'll be distributed. Depending on where you will have your first pictures taken, the florist can come either to your home or to the ceremony site. He or she should arrive before or around the same time as your photographer, since you'll want everyone to have bouquets, boutonnieres, and corsages for all of your pictures. Your flowers should arrive well misted in boxes or wrapped in cellophane. Check to ensure that the right flowers have been delivered. Your florist should inspect each item as soon as possible and remove any bruised or tattered petals. If you don't have a florist present, gently remove the damaged petals yourself, taking care not to disturb the overall shape and look of the bouquet. In order to get all your flowers distributed properly, partner your florist with a close family member who will know the names and faces of all of those receiving flowers. This way you'll avoid confusion, save time, and limit the number of people who handle the flowers.

Keeping Flowers Fresh

Ordering beautiful bouquets is the easy part; keeping them that way takes some effort. For maximum freshness, before the ceremony keep your bouquets out of extreme temperatures; protect them from heat and humidity, and from cold drafts. It's also wise to keep them away from direct sunlight, which can lead to discoloration. Finally, be sure that your blossoms are getting enough water, so they don't wilt before you walk down the aisle. Some nosegays may have their stems anchored in tiny vials of water, but if you have hand-tied bouquets with exposed stems you can keep them in glasses of water right up until the last moment (just be sure to dry them off so the water doesn't stain your gown or the bridesmaids' dresses). If the stems are wrapped, you can mist the heads.

Happy Endings

When all is said and done, you have your wedding band, your gown, your pictures, and maybe a preserved bouquet to remind you of what you felt like as you walked down the aisle. The flowers you fell in love with can continue to play a part in your marriage. Why not start a garden together using a few seedlings or bulbs of these same beloved varieties? If you gave your guests packets of seeds as favors, be sure to plant some yourself. Celebrate your anniversary by giving each other arrangements made of the same varieties as your wedding flowers. For an even longer-lasting memento, plant a tree together when you return from your honeymoon. With each passing year, your tree will grow stronger. It will weather the seasons and provide shade and shelter in times of need. And with nurturing and constant tending, your marriage will do the same.

The Bouquet Toss

The practice of tossing the bouquet dates back to ancient times, when brides would throw flowers in hopes of passing their good fortune on to another woman. Today, of course, it is said that the woman who catches the bouquet will be next to marry. Chances are you won't want to toss your actual bouquet; many brides choose to have a special tossing bouquet made up, similar to the main bridal bouquet but generally smaller and less ornate (and less expensive). Toward the end of the reception, your bandleader or master of ceremonies will call all the single ladies to the dance floor, and you'll turn your back to blindly toss your bouquet over your shoulder to a lucky gal.

If you would rather not toss your bouquet at all, there are certainly alternatives to the tradition. You could opt to give the bouquet to a special friend or relative. If you've lost a loved one, you could honor the person's memory by leaving your bouquet on the grave. Or you could hold the "anniversary dance," where all the married couples join the bride and groom on the dance floor, and as the bandleader or DJ plays a song, couples are eliminated by the number of years they've been married. The last couple left on the dance floor are the people who have been married the longest; they are then presented with the bouquet.

Wedding Day Floral Timeline

Here is a rough guideline for what should happen on your wedding day. Time frames may vary depending on your venues and whether your team of helpers or your florist is delivering and setting up all of your flowers. For a complete timeline of floral tasks leading up to your wedding day, see page 161.

Morning of

- If you are doing your own flowers, create the bouquets. Be sure to keep prepared flowers cool and out of direct sunlight until you're ready to use them. Spritz flowers with water if necessary.

2 to 3 Hours Before

- Your reception flowers should be delivered to the reception site for setup. If you have arranged your own flowers, have a trusted friend transport the arrangements to your ceremony and reception sites well before you (and they) need to start getting dressed.
- Remember to tip the delivery people. Assign the best man or other trusted person to handle this for you.

1 to 2 Hours Before

- Flowers should be delivered to your church or temple for setup.
- Make sure everyone has his or her bouquet, boutonniere, or corsage. If photos are being taken before the ceremony, personal flowers should be handed out then. Otherwise, bouquets don't need to be handed out until right before you head down the aisle. Do-it-yourselfers, simply give a family member a list of those receiving flowers and assign that person the task of distributing them. Learn how to hold a bouquet on page 84, pin on a boutonniere on page 103, and pin on a corsage on page 113.

At the Ceremony

- After greeting your fiancé at the altar, you may pass your bouquet to your maid of honor. In some religious ceremonies, the officiant may place the bouquet on a blessing table. This frees up your hands to exchange the rings and, in Jewish weddings, drink from the kiddush cup.
- Before heading back down the aisle, don't forget to retrieve your bouquet! Caught up in this thrilling moment, many a bride has recessed empty-handed.

At the Reception

- Once you arrived at the reception, you'll want to have your hands free for all of the hugging and greeting that takes place. Traditionally, the bridal bouquet is placed on the cake table. These days, however, brides are opting to display them nearly anywhere, from resting them on the gift or place-card table to setting them in a vase at the head table.
- When the party is winding down, you may want to toss your bouquet (or a specially created tossing bouquet) to your single female friends (opposite).
- If you plan to have your bouquet preserved (see page 166), arrange for your maid of honor or a bridesmaid to handle its transport.

The Next Morning

- If you worked with a florist, he or she will return to the reception site to pick up arrangement holders, such as pots and vases.

FLOWER	SEASON	COLORS	SCENT	MEANING	COST
Alstroemeria *also* Peruvian lily	year-round	white, yellow, orange, pink, red, lavender, purple; flecked	none	n/a	$
Amaryllis	November–April	white, yellow, green, pink, red, burgundy	none (belladonna variety has a mild sweet fragrance)	splendid beauty; pride	$$–$$$
Anemone	November–May; spring is primary season	white, pink, purple, magenta, burgundy	none	expectation	$$–$$$
Aster	November–May in the U.S.; year-round if imported from South America	white, yellow, pink, purple	none	variety; I will partake of your sentiments	$$
Bouvardia	year-round	white, peach, pink, red	faint	enthusiasm	$$
Calla Lily	year-round; winter to late spring is peak	ivory, yellow, orange, light pink, dark pink, red, dark burgundy	none	ardor; magnificent beauty; feminine modesty	$$$
Camellia	late winter–early spring; fall	white, cream, pink, red	mild, sweet	excellence; beauty; perfected loveliness; contentment	$–$$
Carnation	year-round	white, yellow, apricot, pale pink, dark pink, red, burgundy; also bicolors and flecked	spicy, clovelike	admiration; fascination; strong and pure love; unfading beauty	$
Chrysanthemum	year-round; peak in late summer and fall	white, yellow, green, orange, russet, red, burgundy	strong, musky	cheerfulness; optimisim; long life; joy	$
Cockscomb	mid summer–frost	yellow, green, orange, pink, red, crimson	none	n/a	$$
Cornflower	summer–early fall	white, pink, blue	none	delicacy; felicity	$–$$
Cosmos	mid summer–fall	white, pale pink, dark pink	none	modesty	$–$$
Daffodil *also* narcissus/paperwhite, jonquil	November–April	white, yellow, apricot, orange	clean, sweet or none; paperwhite narcissus have a very strong scent	regard; respect; chivalry; gracefulness	$–$$

$ = inexpensive $$ = moderate $$$ = expensive

FLOWER	SEASON	COLORS	SCENT	MEANING	COST
Dahlia	summer–early fall	white, yellow, orange, pink, red, purple	spicy	gratitude; dignity; forever thine	$
Daisy	summer–early fall	white	none to faint	innocence; simplicity; I share your sentiments	$
Delphinium	year-round; peak June–October	white, pink, lavender, purple, blue	none	well-being; sweetness	$$–$$$
Dutch Tulip	November–May	white, yellow, orange, pale pink, dark pink, red, purple	none to mild, sweet scent	declaration of love; honesty; happy years; memory	$–$$
Freesia	year-round	most but blue	very sweet, almost fruity	innocence	$$
French tulip	November–May	ivory, pale yellow, pink	none	n/a	$$$
Gardenia	year-round	ivory	very fragrant perfume	transport of joy; ecstasy; I love you in secret; purity; peace	$$$
Gerbera	year-round	white, yellow, orange, pale pink, dark pink, red	none	needing protection; friendship	$$
Gladiolus *also* sword lily	year-round; peak during summer	white, yellow, green, apricot, orange, pale pink, dark pink, red, lavender, purple	none	generosity; strength of character; you pierce my heart	$
Gloriosa Lily	year-round	red with yellow edges	none	n/a	$$–$$$
Grape Hyacinth *also* Muscari	November–May	white-green, blue-purple	sweet, like grapes or candy	usefulness	$$–$$$
Hyacinth	November–May	white, yellow, peach, pale pink; fuchsia, lavender, purple, blue	very sweet; stronger as florets open	benevolence; play	$$
Hydrangea	July–November	white, green, pink, burgundy, purple, blue	none	devotion; remembrance; boastfulness	$$–$$$
Iris	year-round; peak in spring and early summer	white, yellow, purple	none to sweet depending on variety	message; eloquence; my compliments; promise	$–$$

$ = inexpensive $$ = moderate $$$ = expensive

FLOWER	SEASON	COLORS	SCENT	MEANING	COST
Lady's Mantle	May–November	chartreuse	none	n/a	$$
Larkspur	year-round; peak June–October	white, pink, lavender, purple	none	ardent attachment; levity; swiftness	$$–$$$
Lilac	spring; imported, scentless variety available in November–January	white, pale pink, dark pink, lavender, purple	strong and sweet, except for the winter variety	youth; acceptance; love; beauty; modesty; first emotions of love	$$–$$$
Lily Oriental, Asiatic	year-round; peak in spring and summer	white, yellow, apricot, orange, dark pink; also bicolors and flecked	none to strong depending on variety	purity; fruitfulness; majesty	$$–$$$
Lily of the Valley	available year-round in limited quantities; peak in spring	white, pale pink (rare)	very fragrant	return of happiness; delicacy	$$$
Lisianthus	year-round	white, cream, pale green, peach, pink, lavender, purple	none	showy	$$
Orchid	year-round	white, yellow, green, apricot, orange, pale pink, dark pink, red, burgundy	some varieties are fragrant	luxury; nobility; lust	$$–$$$
Ornithogalum *also* Chincherinchee, Star of Bethlehem	year-round	white, ivory, yellow, orange	slight to none	purity	$$
Parrot Tulip	November–May	white/green, yellow/red, orange/green, pink/green	none	n/a	$$–$$$
Peony	spring; imported varieties available in fall and winter	white, cream, peach, pink, burgundy	sweet and mild to very aromatic	beauty; welcome; bashfulness	$$–$$$
Phlox	June–November	white, orange, pink, red, purple	sweet and mild	Our souls are united; proposal of love; sweet dreams; unanimity	$$
Queen Anne's Lace	spring–early fall	white, green	grassy scent	haven; protection; I'll return	$

$ = inexpensive $$ = moderate $$$ = expensive

FLOWER	SEASON	COLORS	SCENT	MEANING	COST
Ranunculus	November–April	white, yellow, apricot, orange, pale pink, dark pink	mild	You are rich in attractions; I am dazzled by your charms	$$-$$$
Rose	year-round	white, cream, yellow, apricot, orange, russet, pale pink, dark pink, red, burgundy, lavender	none to intense, depending on the variety	several meanings depending on color; generally: love; beauty grace; joy; unity	$$-$$$
Scabiosa	spring–early fall	white, burgundy, lavender	none	sensible woman	$$-$$$
Stephanotis	year-round	white	slight	Will you accompany me?	$$$
Stock	year-round; peak in spring and summer	white, yellow, apricot, pale pink, dark pink, purple	strong, spicy clove scent	promptness; lasting beauty	$
Sunflower	May–November; peak in summer	pale lemon, deep gold, orange, russet, brown	none	loyalty; adoration; pride	$$
Sweet Pea	November–June	white, cream, apricot, pale pink, dark pink, red, lavender, purple	intense, sweet fragrance	everlasting pleasures	$$-$$$
Tuberose	summer–fall	ivory-pink	very strong perfume	dangerous love; voluptuousness	$$-$$$
Tweedia	April–November	blue	none	n/a	$$
Veronica	year-round	white, pink, purple	none	fidelity	$-$$
Viburnum	November–May	white, green	slight fragrance	good news; jubilation	$$-$$$
Zinnia	June–September	yellow, green, orange, pink, red	none	thoughts of friends	$

$ = inexpensive $$ = moderate $$$ = expensive

PRESERVING YOUR BOUQUET

Your bouquet can be the perfect wedding keepsake. To preserve it, you'll need to choose a method and find someone who can do it for you long before you walk down the aisle. Not all flowers are suitable for preservation; talk to your preservationist about the varieties you plan to have in your bouquet.

There are several ways to preserve a bouquet, but different techniques have varying costs and varying levels of success, depending on the flowers. Regardless of which method you choose, it's best to keep your bouquet as fresh as possible after your wedding, either by setting it in water if it has exposed stems or by misting it and storing it in the fridge (not the freezer). If you're heading out of town immediately afterward, enlist a friend or family member to keep your bouquet fresh and deliver it to your preservationist. Here are four common preservation techniques.

Pressing: This simple method is a wonderful do-it-yourself way to preserve select blossoms from your bouquet. Flowers with thinner petals will work best. First, remove any visible sign of moisture from the blooms, and place a few sheets of absorbent paper on a flat surface or the bottom of a flower press. Lay the flowers on the paper and cover with more paper. Flatten the pile using pressure from heavy objects, such as bricks or books, or from the top of the press, and keep in a warm, dry location. Once the flowers are dried, frame them or use them in craft projects.

Air-drying: This easy, do-it-yourself technique works well for nearly all flowers, particularly roses. Keep in mind that the blossoms will shrink and fade, and may even blacken. If you have a tight cluster bouquet, remove some of the stems to allow for better air circulation. Simply hang the blooms upside down in a warm, dry environment and not too much light. Within a couple of days to several weeks, depending on the flowers, you should have a bouquet of dried blossoms.

Silver sand and silica gel: This method works on nearly every type of flower but requires the help of an expert. The flowers are submerged in a drying medium, either silver sand or silica gel, which holds the petals in place as they dry. Depending on the flower variety the process can take anywhere from a few days to a couple of weeks. Although expensive, this method results in very true-to-life flowers that keep their shape and color.

Freeze-drying: Though costly, this professional technique produces the most lifelike results. The flowers are deep-frozen in a special double-chambered container, then covered in a protective coating. Nearly any type of flower can be preserved this way.

Was there an idea you'd like to use or a bouquet you loved in this book? Contact information is listed below for the florists, event planners, and others whose work we have featured (see pages 175 to 176 for specific credits) or whose expertise we have consulted. To get the latest wedding flower information, to view The Knot Flower Galleries, or to find a florist in your area, log on to:
www.theknot.com/flowers

FLORISTS AND EVENT PLANNERS

Avi Adler
New York, NY • 718-243-0804
www.aviadler.com

Belle Fleur
New York, NY • 212-254-8703
www.bellefleurny.com

Bloom
New York, NY • 212-620-5666
www.bloomflowers.com

Blumen
Chicago, IL • 312-666-7304

Botanica, Inc.
New York, NY • 212-563-9013
www.botanicainc.com

Botanicals, Inc.
Chicago, IL • 773-342-5165

Color of Magic
New York, NY • 212-967-5439

The Daily Blossom
New York, NY • 212-633-9000

Details
St. Louis, MO • 636-230-6426

Elizabeth Ryan
New York, NY • 212-995-1111
www.erflowers.com

Events of Distinction
San Francisco, CA
415-751-0211 • 866-99-EVENT
www.eventsofdistinction.com

Flowers From The Woods Inc.
Atlanta, GA • 404-347-8086

The Gallery Flowers & Gifts
Petersburg, VA • 804-732-3980

Leslie Palme Event Design
New York, NY • 212-643-9059

Lotus NYC
New York, NY • 212-463-0555
www.nycflowers.com

Mandana Flowers
New York, NY • 212-643-6771

Martha E. Harris
Seattle, WA • 206-568-0347

Matthew David Events, Ltd.
New York, NY • 212-627-2086
www.matthewdavidevents.com

Michael George
New York, NY • 212-751-0689
www.michaelgeorgecustomfloral.com

Peter M. Krask Design
by appointment
New York, NY • 212-568-0346
pmkrask@aol.com

Preston Bailey Design
New York, NY • 212-691-6777

Quade Events and Design
Brooklyn, NY • 718-788-8355
www.quadedesigns.com

Rebecca Cole
New York, NY • 212-929-3210
www.colecreates.com

RENNY: Design for Entertaining
New York, NY • 212-288-7000
www.rennydesign.com

stonekelly events - florals
New York, NY • 212-245-6611
www.stonekelly.com

Susan Holland & Co.
Event Design and Catering
New York, NY • 212-807-8892
www.susanholland.com

through the grapevine
Washington, DC • 202-547-5093
www.ttgflowers.com

VSF
New York, NY • 212-206-7236

WEDDING PLANNERS

Elegant Occasions
New York, NY
212-704-0048 • 888-361-9177
www.elegantoccasions.com

Jean Picard
Los Angeles/Orange County/
Santa Barbara, CA • 805-642-3201

Melissa Paul Ltd.
Philadelphia, PA • 610-293-9550
www.melissapaul.com

FLOWER PRESERVATION

Aiko & Co.
Nationwide • 877-245-6626
www.pressed-bouquet.com

Floral Techniques
Nationwide • 408-266-2425
lorraine@floraltechniques.com
www.floraltechniques.com

Florescence
Washington, DC • 301-681-6066
www.preservemyflowers.com

Forever In Bloom
Mt. Kisco, NY
914-241-1963 • 888-404-3837
www.foreverinbloomonline.com

Forever In Bloom, Inc.
Chicago, IL • 630-837-3668
www.fibinc.com

Garden Bouquet Floral Preservation
Southern CA • 805-498-5098
www.bouquetpreservation.com

Heller & Reid
Nationwide • 800-742-9570
www.hellerandreid.com

The Floral Portrait
Nationwide • 800-771-7560
www.thefloralportrait.com

PROFESSIONAL SOCIETIES

American Institute of Floral Designers
410-752-3318
www.aifd.org
Accrediting advanced professional
floral design artists; more than 1200
members

Society of American Florists
Nationwide • 800-336-4743
www.aboutflowers.com
The national trade association for the
floral industry

FLORAL SUPPLIES AND TOOLS

Frank's Nursery & Crafts, Inc.
Midwest
www.franksnursery.com

JoAnn Fabrics & Crafts
Nationwide
www.joann.com

Michaels
Nationwide • 800-MICHAELS
www.michaels.com

GROWER'S BUNCHES

Big Rose
www.bigrose.com

Bridal Blooms & Creations
www.bridalblooms.com

Chelsea Wholesale Flower Market
New York, NY • 212-620-7500

Costco
Nationwide • 800-774-2678
www.costco.com

Flower Resource Directory
www.flowersource.net

Flowerbud
www.flowerbud.com

The International Flower Market
www.iflowermarket.com

24 Roses
www.24roses.com

WEDDING FASHION

To view more than 20,000 pictures of gowns, visit www.theknot.com/gowns

Wearkstatt
New York, NY • 212-279-3929
www.wearkstattbridal.com

Cose Belle
New York, NY • 212-988-4210

Jim Hjelm Occasions
Nationwide • 800-686-7880
www.jimhjelmoccasions.com

Lazaro
New York, NY • 212-764-5781
www.lazarobridal.com/bridesmaid

Serafina
New York, NY • 212-253-2754
www.serafina.net

Simple Silhouettes
New York, NY • 212-598-3030
www.simpledress.com

Thread Bridesmaid
New York, NY • 212-414-8844
www.threaddesign.com

Vanessa Noel Shoes
New York, NY • 212-906-0054
www.vanno.com

CALLIGRAPHERS

Sharon Arditty Calligraphy & Design
Queens, NY • 718-544-3853

Margaret Neiman Harber,
Kaleidakolor Calligraphy
New York, NY • 212-475-1653

Kathryn Shaughnessy, Calligraphics
New York, NY • 917-856-7615

OTHER RESOURCES

ASAP Linens
New York, NY • 212-243-4400
Wide range of rental table linens for weddings and events

Bridalink Store
www.bridalink.com
Favor supplies, miniature galvanized buckets, tussy mussies, personalized items, and ceremony supplies.

Broadway Famous Party Rentals
Brooklyn, NY • 718-821-4000
Rental tables, chairs, place settings, and linens for weddings and events

The Chelsea Paper Company
www.chelseapaper.com
Stationery for all occasions

Ephemera Studio
718-384-3513
Fine soy candles with botanical oils

Gail Watson Custom Cakes
New York, NY • 212-967-9167

Ice Fantasies Inc.
Nationwide • 800-NICE-ICE
www.icefantasies.com
Custom ice design

Krisztina Webber
New York, NY • 212-243-3769
Makeup design for all occasions

Plant a Memory
www.plantamemory.com
Seeds and bulbs for favors

Ruth Fischl
New York, NY • 212-273-9710
www.ruthfischl.com
Designer linens and prop rental for weddings and events

Soho Studios
New York, NY • 212-226-1100
man-lai@sohostudios.com
www.sohostudios.com
Loft space available for weddings, rehearsal dinners, and parties

Smith & Hawken
800-940-1170
www.smithandhawken.com
Bulbs for favors and florist supplies

Sylvia Weinstock Cakes
New York, NY • 212-925-6698

Tri Serve Party Rental
New York, NY • 212-752-7661
Glassware, flatware, and china for weddings and events

Resources from The Knot

You'll find lots of helpful information in our magazines and on our Web site, www.theknot.com

IDEAS AND INSPIRATION: View our flower galleries and read about the latest floral trends at www.theknot.com/flowers

FLORISTS: Find local florists in your area at www.theknot.com/local and in *The Knot Weddingpages* magazine for your region

WEDDING SUPPLIES: Shop for flower girl baskets, tussy mussies, and more in our on-line store at www.theknot.com/store

Angeloni, Umberto. *The Boutonniere: Style in One's Lapel.* New York: Universe Publishing, 2000.

Appell, Scott D. *Lilies.* New York: Friedman/Fairfax Publishers, 2000.

Bales, Suzy. *A Garden of Fragrance.* New York: Regan Books, 2000.

Barrett, Jean T., and Colin Cowie. *Colin Cowie Weddings.* New York: Little, Brown and Company, 1998.

Blum, Marcy, and Laura Fisher Kaiser. *Weddings for Dummies.* Foster City, Calif.: IDG Books Worldwide, 1997.

Brennan, Georgeann. *Flowerkeeping.* Berkeley, Calif.: Ten Speed Press, 1999.

Connolly, Shane. *Shane Connolly's Wedding Flowers.* North Pomfret, VT: Trafalgar Square Publishing, 1998.

Donzel, Catherine. *The Book of Flowers.* Paris: Flammarion, 1998.

Edelkoort, Li. *Bloom Book: Horticulture for the 21st Century.* Paris: Flammarion, 2001.

Forsell, Mary. *Victoria Romantic Weddings.* New York: William Morrow and Company, 1998.

Girand-Lagorce, Sylvie. *The Book of Roses.* Paris: Flammarion, 2001.

Guth, Tracy. *For Your Wedding: Flowers.* New York: Michael Friedman Publishing Company, 2000.

Heckman, Marsha. *Bouquets: A Year of Flowers for the Bride.* New York: Stewart, Tabori & Chang, 2000.

Heffernan, Cecelia. *Flowers A to Z.* New York: Harry N. Abrams, Inc., 2001.

Heilmeyer, Marina. *The Language of Flowers: Symbols and Myths.* London, New York: Prestel Verlag, 2001.

Laufer, Geraldine Adamich. *Tussie-Mussies: The Victorian Art of Expressing Yourself in the Language of Flowers.* New York: Workman Publishing Company, 1993.

Lemmers, Willem. *Tulipa.* New York: Artisan, 1999.

Lipanovich, Marianne, ed. *Sunset Orchids.* Menlo Park, Calif.: Sunset Books, 1999.

McBride-Mellinger, Maria. *Bridal Flowers: Arrangements for the Perfect Wedding.* New York: Bulfinch Press, 1992.

—— *The Perfect Wedding Reception.* New York: HarperCollins Publishers, 2001.

—— *The Perfect Wedding.* New York: Collins Publishers, 1997.

Monckton, Shirley. *The Complete Book of Wedding Flowers.* London: The Cassell Wellington House, 1995.

Norden, Mary. *Wedding Details.* New York: HarperCollins, 2000.

Packer, Jane. *Flowers, Design, Philosophy.* London: Conran Octopus Limited, 2000.

Perry, Clay. *A World of Flowers.* New York: St. Martin's Press, 2001.

Pickles, Sheila. *The Language of Flowers.* New York: Harmony Books, 1990.

Pryke, Paula. *Flair with Flowers.* New York: Rizzoli International Publications, 1995.

—— *Flowers Flowers.* New York: Rizzoli International Publications, 1993.

—— *Simple Flowers.* New York: Rizzoli International Publications, 1999.

Rogers, Ray, and Beth Smiley, eds. *Ultimate Rose (American Rose Society).* New York: Dorling Kindersley Publishing, Inc., 2000.

Seaton, Beverly. *The Language of Flowers: A History.* Charlottesville, VA: The University Press of Virginia, 1995.

Tonks, Diana. *Flowers on Your Wedding Day.* Chicago: Contemporary Books, 1994.

Tortu, Christian. *Sensational Arrangements.* New York: Harry N. Abrams, Inc., 2001.

Wells, Diana. *100 Flowers and How They Got Their Names.* Chapel Hill, NC: Algonquin Books of Chapel Hill, 1997.

A

Air-drying, 166
Albert (prince), 8
Alstroemeria, 12, 162
Altar arrangement, 130
Amaryllis, 12, 162
Anemone, 12, 162
Antony, Marc, 38
Arch decorations, 130, 134
Argentina, 67
Arum lily. *See* Calla lily
Asiatic lily, 28, 164
Aster, 15, 68, 162
Australia, 67

B

Bailey, Preston, 155
Bearded iris, 25
Berries, 49, 65
Biedermeier bouquet, 84, 95
Birth month flowers, 68
Blue color palette, 56
Bouquets. *See also individual types*
    embellishing, 109
    keeping fresh, 160
    preserving, 166
    shapes of, 94-95, 97
Boutonnieres, 100-105
    cost of, 64
    do-it-yourself, 104-5
    history of, 8
    pinning, 103
Bouvardia, 15, 162
Branches, 49
Breakaway centerpiece, 127
Bridal bouquet, 84-99
    color of, 84
    cost of, 64
    do-it-yourself, 98-99
    gown and, 84, 87
    history of, 7
    holding, 84
    shape of, 94-95, 97
    size of, 84, 87
    style of, 89-90, 93
Bridesmaids' bouquets, 64, 106-9
Budget, 65

C

Caesar, Julius, 38
Cake decorations, 137-38
Calendula, 68
Calla lily, 15, 162
Camellia, 16, 72, 162
Candelabra centerpiece, 124
Canopy decorations, 134
Carnation, 16, 68, 162
Cascade bouquet, 95
Ceibo, 67
Centerpieces, 115-29
    cost of, 64
    do-it-yourself, 128-29
    games with, 116
    height of, 116
    shapes of, 124, 127
    styles of, 119-20, 123
Ceremony. *See* Scene setters; Timeline
Chair decorations, 133-34
Chile, 67
China, 67, 72
Chincherinchee, 164
Chrysanthemum, 16, 68, 72, 162
Cleopatra, 38
Cockscomb, 162
Color palettes
    blue and purple, 56
    choosing, 67
    pink, 52
    red and orange, 55
    white, 51
    yellow and green, 59
Composite bouquet, 97
Confucius, 16
Copihue, 67
Cornflower, 18, 162
Corsages, 113
    cost of, 64
    pinning, 113

Cosmos, 18, 162
Cost, 64, 65, 162–65
Cymbidium orchid, 33, 34

D

Daffodil, 18, 68, 162
Dahlia, 19, 163
Daisy, 8, 19, 163
Decorations. *See* Scene setters
Delphinium, 19, 163
Dendrobium orchid, 34
Denmark, 72
Do-it-yourself flowers, 75–77
    boutonniere, 104–5
    bridal bouquet, 98–99
    centerpiece, 128–29
Dutch iris, 25
Dutch tulip, 46, 163

E

Edelweiss, 67
Edward VIII (king), 8
Egypt, 67
England, 67

F

Fall weddings, 150, 153
Faux flowers, 65
Favors, 138
Finland, 67
Florists
    celebrity, 8
    contract with, 71–72
    finding, 69–72
    working with, 159–60
Flower girl's blooms, 110
    cost of, 64
    history of, 7
Formal weddings, 62
Fragrant flowers, 68
France, 67
Freesia, 21, 163
Freeze-drying, 166
French tulip, 45, 46, 163

G

Gardenia, 21, 72, 163
Garlands, 134
George, Michael, 147
Gerbera, 21, 163
Gift table arrangements, 137
Gladiolus, 22, 68, 163
Globe centerpiece, 127
Gloriosa lily, 28, 163
Golden wattle, 67
Gown, 64, 84, 87
Grape hyacinth, 22, 163
Greeks, ancient, 7, 72, 110
Green color palette, 59
Greenery, 49

H

Herbs, 49, 65, 72
Hibiscus, 67
History, 7–9
Huppah, 134
Hyacinth, 22, 72, 163
Hydrangea, 25, 163

I

India, 67, 72
Informal weddings, 62
Iris, 25, 163
Italy, 72
Ivy, 65, 72

J

Japan, 72
Jonquil, 18, 162
Josephine (empress), 19

L

Lady's mantle, 164
Language of flowers, 8, 110, 162–65
Larkspur, 19, 68, 164
Lilac, 8, 25, 164
Lilies, 27–28, 67
    Asiatic, 28, 164
    calla, 15, 45, 162

gloriosa, 28, 163
longiflorum, 28
Oriental, 27, 164
Peruvian, 12, 162
sword, 163
of the valley, 30, 67, 68, 164
Lisianthus, 30, 65, 164
Longiflorum lily, 28
Lotus, 67

M

Madonna lily, 28
Mary, Virgin, 27, 28
Maximilian of Austria, 16
Monet, Claude, 25
Mudan, 67
Muscari, 163

N

Narcissus, 18, 68, 162
National flowers, 67
National traditions, 72
Nero, 38
Netherlands, 67
Nosegay, 94

O

Oncidium orchid, 34
Orange color palette, 55
Orchids, 33–34, 164
    cymbidium, 33, 34
    dendrobium, 34
    oncidium, 34
    phalaenopsis, 34
Oriental lily, 27, 164
Ornithogalum, 164

P

Pageant bouquet, 97
Paperwhite narcissus, 18, 162
Parakeet tulip. *See* Parrot tulip
Parks, Saundra, 150
Parrot tulip, 46, 164
Pedestal centerpiece, 127

Peony, 37, 72, 164
Peruvian lily, 12, 162
Pew-end decorations, 133
Phalaenopsis orchid, 34
Philippines, 67
Phlox, 37, 164
Pink color palette, 52
Place-card table arrangements, 137
Pomander, 97
Posy, 94
Prayer book, 87
Presentation bouquet, 97
Pressing, 166
Puerto Rico, 67
Purple color palette, 56

Q
Queen Anne's lace, 164

R
Ranunculus, 37, 165
Reception. *See* Scene setters; Timeline
Red color palette, 55
Rembrandt tulip. *See* Parrot tulip
Reynolds, Renny, 142
Romans, ancient, 7, 110
Rosemary, 49
Roses, 38–41, 67, 68, 165
    garden, 41
    hybrid tea, 41
    spray, 41
    symbolism of, 8

S
Sampaguita, 67
Sample weddings
    spring, 142, 145
    summer, 147–48
    fall, 150, 153
    winter, 155–56
Scabiosa, 42, 165
Scene setters, 130–38
    altar arrangement, 130
    arch decorations, 130, 134

cake decorations, 137–38
chair decorations, 133–34
cost of, 64
favors and finishing touches, 138
gift table arrangements, 137
huppah and canopy
    decorations, 134
pew-end decorations, 133
place-card table
    arrangements, 137
recycling, 65
wreaths and garlands, 134
Season, 64, 65, 162–65
Semiformal weddings, 62
Shakespeare, William, 18
Shower bouquet, 95
Siberian iris, 25
Silica gel, 166
Silk flowers, 65
Silver sand, 166
Simpson, Wallis, 8
Site, appearance of, 62, 64
South Africa, 67
Spending guide, 64
Spray centerpiece, 124
Spring weddings, 142, 145
Spry, Constance, 8
Star of Bethlehem, 164
Stein, Gertrude, 38
Stem treatments, 77
Stephanotis, 42, 165
Stock, 42, 165
Style considerations, 67–68
Summer weddings, 147–48
Sunflower, 43, 72, 165
Sweden, 72
Sweet pea, 43, 68, 165
Switzerland, 67
Sword lily, 163

T
Tahiti, 67
Thailand, 72
Themes, 68

Tiare, 67
Tiered centerpiece, 124
Timeline, 78–79, 161
Tossing bouquet, 160
    cost of, 64
    history of, 7
Trumpet centerpiece, 124
Tuberose, 43, 165
Tulips, 45–46, 67
    Dutch, 46, 163
    French, 45, 46, 163
    parrot, 46, 164
Turkey, 67
Tussy mussy, 110
Tweedia, 48, 165

U
United States of America,
    national flower of, 67

V
Van Gogh, Vincent, 25
Verdi, Giuseppe, 16
Veronica, 48, 165
Viburnum, 165
Victoria (queen), 8, 110
Violet, 68

W
Weather, 64
Wedding day, tips for, 159–60
White color palette, 51
Winter weddings, 155–56
Wordsworth, William, 18
Worksheet, 80–81
Wreaths, 134

Y
Yellow color palette, 59

Z
Zinnia, 48, 165

CREDITS

Here's a page-by-page list of the flowers that appear throughout the book. Look to the Resources section (pages 167–169) for the floral designers' numbers and Web sites, where applicable. For the most up-to-date wedding flower designs and vendor contacts, log on to www.theknot.com/flowers, where you'll find floral information and inspiration 24/7.

All photographs by Wendell Webber unless otherwise noted.

PAGE	CREDIT
Cover	Bouquet by Elizabeth Ryan. gown by Wearkstatt
2	Bouquet by The Daily Blossom; gown by Wearkstatt; photograph by Troy House
6	Bouquet by Elizabeth Ryan
10	Bouquet by Leslie Palme Event Design
12	Alstroemeria bouquet by Botanica
16	Camellia photo: © Peter Smithers / CORBIS
18	Cosmos photo: © W. Wayne Lockwood M.D. / CORBIS Daffodil bouquet by Botanica
19	Dahlia photo: Getty Images / Davies & Starr
20	Gardenia bouquet by Peter M. Krask; photograph by Paul Costello
32	Bouquet by The Daily Blossom; photograph by Troy House
39	Bouquet by Peter M. Krask; photograph by Paul Costello
44	Bouquet by Peter M. Krask; photograph by Paul Costello
48	Tweedia boutonniere by Peter M. Krask; photograph by Paul Costello
49	Boutonniere by Peter M. Krask; photograph by Paul Costello
50	Bouquet by VSF
53	Bouquet by Peter M. Krask; photograph by Paul Costello
54	Bouquet by Peter M. Krask; photograph by Paul Costello
57	Bouquet by Peter M. Krask; photograph by Paul Costello
58	Bouquet by Quade
60	Bouquet by Lotus NYC; gown by Wearkstatt; photograph by Troy House
63	Bouquet by Lotus NYC; gown by Wearkstatt; photograph by Troy House
66	Bouquet by Botanica; gown by Wearkstatt; photograph by Troy House
73	Bouquet by Elizabeth Ryan
78	Bouquet by The Daily Blossom; photograph by Troy House
82	Boutonniere by Elizabeth Ryan
85	Bouquet by Elizabeth Ryan
86	Bouquet by Rebecca Cole; gown by Wearkstatt

PAGE	CREDIT	PAGE	CREDIT	PAGE	CREDIT
88	Stephanotis bouquet by Leslie Palme Event Design; Rose bouquet by Peter M. Krask, photograph by Paul Costello; Tulip bouquet by Elizabeth Ryan; Calla lily bouquet by Peter M. Krask, photograph by Paul Costello	108	Bridesmaids: Orange ranunculus bouquet by Elizabeth Ryan, dress by Thread; Lavender dress by Simple Silhouettes; Pink peony bouquet by Elizabeth Ryan, dress by Laundry; Orchid bouquet by Elizabeth Ryan, dress by Lazaro	124-127	All centerpieces by Matthew David Events, Ltd.
91	Tweedia and ranunculus bouquet by Quade; Baby's breath bouquet by Peter M. Krask, photograph by Paul Costello; Hydrangea and camomile bouquet by Peter M. Krask, photograph by Paul Costello; Sunflower bouquet by Peter M. Krask, photograph by Paul Costello	111	Flower girl basket by The Knot Wedding Collections available at www.theknot.com/shop	129	Centerpiece by Peter M. Krask
		112	Corsage by VSF	131	Archway by Lotus NYC
		114	Centerpiece and place setting by Lotus NYC	132	Ceremony arrangement by Lotus NYC
		117	Centerpiece by stonekelly events - florals	133	Chair back by Lotus NYC
92	Red rose and calla lily bouquet by Rebecca Cole; Rose and hydrangea bouquet by Peter M. Krask, photograph by Paul Costello; Rose and sweet pea bouquet by Rebecca Cole; Cascade bouquet by Elizabeth Ryan; gown by Wearkstatt	118	Rose and hydrangea centerpiece by Peter M. Krask; White anthurium centerpiece by Susan Holland & Co.; Ornithogalum arabicum and wheat grass centerpiece by Mandana Flowers; Rose pedestal centerpiece by Bloom	134	White favor pail available from www.bridalink.com
				135	Reception arrangement by Peter M. Krask
				137	Bulbs from Smith & Hawken
94-97	All bouquets by Color of Magic; gown by Wearkstatt	121	Orchid and hydrangea centerpiece by Color of Magic; Rose, peony, and calla lily breakaway centerpiece by Susan Holland & Co.; Peony and scabiosa centerpiece by The Daily Blossom; Still-life pedestal centerpiece by stonekelly events - florals	138	Floral cake by Gail Watson Custom Cakes
99	Bouquet by Peter M. Krask			139	Cake by Sylvia Weinstock Cakes; Table setting and flowers by Preston Bailey Design
101	Boutonniere by Peter M. Krask; photograph by Paul Costello			143-149	All Spring Wedding flowers by RENNY: Design for Entertaining
102	Boutonnieres Peter M. Krask; photographs by Paul Costello			146-149	All Summer Wedding flowers by Michael George
105	Boutonniere by Peter M. Krask	122	Amaryllis centerpiece by Mandana Flowers; Rose, delphinium, and ranunculus centerpiece by Peter M. Krask; Sunflower centerpiece by stonekelly events - florals; Orchid and pod centerpiece Susan Holland & Co.	151-152	All Fall Wedding flowers by The Daily Blossom
107	Bridesmaid bouquet by Elizabeth Ryan; dress by Jim Hjelm Occasions			154-157	All Winter Wedding flowers by Preston Bailey Design
				158	Bouquet by The Daily Blossom; gown by Wearkstatt; photograph by Troy House

ALSTROEMERIA APARTERIS AN
AMELLIA CARNATION CHRYS
AFFODIL DAHLIA DAISY DELPH
LADIOLUS GRAPE HYACINTH
LY LISIANTHUS ORCHID PEON
EPHANOTIS STOCK SUNFLOV
RONICA ZINNIA ALSTROEME
ALLA LILY CAMELLIA CARNAT
OSMOS DAFFODIL DAHLIA DA
LADIOLUS GRAPE HYACINTH
LY LISIANTHUS ORCHID PEON
EPHANOTIS STOCK SUNFLOV
RONICA ZINNIA ALSTROEME
ALLA LILY CAMELLIA CARNAT
OSMOS DAFFODIL DAHLIA DA
LADIOLUS GRAPE HYACINTH